Like a River Flows

Hanna Grace

To the Kraker family, and of course, to Grandma.

Contents

I
Source

Visit #1

My grandma visited me after she died.

She was sitting on our deck at night, the yard and surrounding houses completely invisible. Only she could be seen, illuminated by golden outdoor lights strung around the deck. Her blonde hair was down around her shoulders, the curls having mostly fallen out, but there were some slight waves giving evidence that they had been there. She was beaming, her laughter the only sound I could hear as her arms remained outstretched, awaiting a hug as I gazed at her.

I never received that hug. I only saw the possibility.

I woke up with tears streaming down my face.

Unable to fall back asleep, I got out of bed and went to the family computer, a white mac that had reached the point of being considered a dinosaur. It took forever to turn on and load the applications, but after waiting patiently I finally got to open iPhoto and begin my search. After seeing my grandma in my dream, I was desperate to see her again by looking at pictures of her, hoping to find a picture of her and me that I had never seen before; but unfortunately, after scrolling through all of them, I was unsuccessful in my search and went back to bed.

Later on in the morning, I told my dad about my dream.

"I had a dream about Grandma last night," I said tentatively. My dad normally cuts off conversations about her short. He is the poster child for the term "mama's boy" and struggles every day with the fact that she's gone.

To my surprise, he answered positively and with more than one word: "That means she was visiting you."

Encouraged, I kept talking. "She was sitting on our deck at night with all the lights on and she was laughing, trying to give me a hug."

"My parents loved sitting on the deck," he replied. And that was it.

My dream being a visit from her sounded wacko to me at first, as the idea that dreams have meanings seemed spooky and supernatural. Besides, my dreams are nothing but weird and confusing: for example, I recently dreamed that the Dodgers and the Patriots played each other in the Super Bowl, and the Dodgers won. But the more I thought about it, the more right he seemed to be. This dream didn't seem random and unrealistic like my other dreams. Like my dad said, Grandma loved sitting on decks, and she came to me the way she always greeted me when she was alive: laughing and smiling, with arms outstretched.

I want to see you clearly, come closer than this.

Trust in the Lord with all your heart

Dear Grandma,

The bottom drawer of my dresser is opened on only two days of the year: June twenty-fifth, your birthday, and August twentieth, the day you died. Inside of it are all of the things I've ever gotten from you, aside from some jewelry and a pink plastic baton that has confetti swirling inside of it, which for some reason, I keep propped up inside a pair of rain boots in my closet. Everything in it is invaluable to me but there is one thing that I put above the rest, the first thing I would save if my house caught on fire: the journal you started for me while I was rapidly forming and growing in my mother's womb, which you gave to me when I was 9 years old to complete on my own. You did this for all of your grandchildren, aside from Kyra and Isaiah, who were born after you died.

Just that detail right there, the fact that you took the initiative to start a journal for all your grandkids, to document parts of our lives that we can't remember and tell us how you felt about all of it — I don't know anyone else who has done something like that. Someone who doesn't just think of the present moment but thinks of us years from now, no longer babies but kids who are growing and developing minds of their own, changing more and more every day and realizing how a journal like that, an account of a grandmother awaiting the arrival of her grandchildren and watching them grow up, could be valuable to us.

In the light of your death, these journals are treasured all the more, as it's like we all have our own pieces of you to hold onto. You gave us a way of hearing your voice again and a way to be reminded of your love for us, the invaluable ability to access you even though you're gone.

I can't and won't open the drawer now, being that it's January thirteenth. But I don't need that journal in my hands to be able to see the two gray wolves on the cover, one howling at the sky and the other laying down, staring off into space and the flurry of snow falling around them, swirling lines indicating wind drawn across the page. On a side note, I'd like to know where you bought your journals; I've seen the other journals for your grandkids and none of them look the same.

And I certainly don't need to go into the drawer because I can picture your handwriting, that beautiful, loopy cursive that people still remark on, almost ten years after your death. I don't need to open that journal and read because the words you wrote to me are ingrained into my brain: the way you described how excited my parents were to have me, how you wished my newborn eyes would stay blue, how you wrote "praise God from Whom all blessings flow" followed by multiple exclamation marks.

You wrote about me and loved me before you knew me. You wrote about me when I wasn't even alive yet, so here I am to write to you even though you aren't alive. I'm going to write to you, because I knew you for ten years but I still feel like I don't know enough about you. And I will write because I only open my drawer full of memories of you only two times a year. Because that drawer is all I have, and within that drawer, within your life and the experiences I've had with and without you, there are stories to tell.
Love,
Hanna Grace

Why I can't use Familytreetemplates.net

This doesn't feel like my story to tell.

Our family tree is huge, containing branches that I know nothing about and heights I've never gotten to climb, a history and future that seem endless. For the sake of this story, I have to narrow it down and look at a more condensed family tree that begins with my grandma, who leads to my dad, who leads to me.

But family trees, as generated by the internet, don't display lineage that way. They put you, the user, at the base, the rest of your family fanning out as the branches. An accurate tree for my family would not begin with me— it would begin with my grandma.

Born Lucinda Faye Haney, known throughout her life as Sandie, she was the seed planted in the ground on June 25, 1948. Within the family I grew up with and the family tree I know best, she is the roots, the foundation.

My dad, the oldest son born in 1966, and the rest of his siblings, the trunk that grows from the seed.

And then me, born in 1998, one tiny branch tucked in there.

It still doesn't feel like it's my story to tell. I feel too small, insignificant.

This is a tree of grandeur and abundance, not some tiny, poor-excuse of a tree like the ones planted in new housing developments. Ours is a tree made up of personalities, hereditary traits, names and souls, all people who go back to her. The branches spread out as we grow and live our lives, but we're still the tree. We go through life together, face the elements, still we all come from the same seed. She is cause for every one of us.

From the one seed we have grown and stretched higher, and will continue to grow, our branches climbing upwards, our roots remaining firmly planted. Towering and unmovable, a family has grown. Our leaves bloom, changing from green to brilliant fire, fall to the ground and then bloom again, and still our tree stands. The sun shines, the snow falls, the wind blows, and still our tree stands.

This doesn't feel like my story to tell, as I am just a branch on a tree that endured and grew from decades of memories and struggles that I didn't experience. I am not the roots, I am not the trunk, I am not a limb that someone could climb and sit on. I only knew the seed for ten years and never dug deep enough to really know or see her. But I'm going to tell it because I'm still here, a branch on the tree, visible evidence of the invisible seed in the ground. And if I don't tell the story, who will?

Sandie is out of sight, buried in the ground. But this seed, this wife, mother, grandmother, woman of many names, never will be gone. Her story lives on, rooted into the ground, scratched into the bark, flowing through the veins of every leaf, stretching towards the sky.

June 25, 2008

I remember my grandma's sixtieth birthday in a blur of sunshine, food, people, and music.

It was a perfect day of Ohio summer: no rain and not too hot, which was a detail that I didn't appreciate as a kid. Adults were the ones who planned the parties and worried about being prepared for all circumstances; the kids just had to help unload the car. I spent most of this party soaking in the sun on the playground nestled in the very back corner of Uncle Joe and Aunt Natalie's backyard, horrified as my cousin, Matt, always fearless, walked across the wooden beam that the swings hung from.

The theme of the party was a Hawaiian Luau and in keeping with that theme, we roasted a pig. Already a very picky eater at that age, I was grossed out after seeing the pig hanging over the fire, and I didn't eat any. I remember a second or third cousin of mine calling dibs on the ears, because apparently they're the best part.

There were so many guests. Of course the aunts, uncles, and cousins that I saw all the time were there, but also the more distant relatives whose names I had a hard time remembering were at the party. Beyond family, it seemed like our entire church was there. The kids played by the playground or the trampoline, the adults hung out around the pig or on the deck by the house, where Grandma, the reason for all this celebration, was sitting in her rollator, her walking aid that looked like a cross between a wheelchair and walker. Most of the guests wore Hawaiian attire, whether it was simply a lei or they went all out with a Hulu skirt or flower-print shirt. Grandma wore a typical Hawaiian, flowered shirt and an orange lei, a constant smile on her face.

One side of the deck was set up as a stage with speakers and music equipment. My dad, Uncle Bill, Uncle Joe, and other musicians from church played music. Grandma was sitting in the front row, listening and talking with guests. Behind her, I remember Aunt Kelly sitting on Uncle Chris's lap, Grandma's third-born son.

With the weather, all of the people and food, the band playing, leis around everyone's neck, it seemed like the party was complete. But it wasn't: my aunts had planned a surprise.

Elvis entered the building.

At least, a local Elvis impersonator came around the side of the house and walked onto the deck.

I wish I could have seen Grandma's initial

reaction when he came out, but I was among the crowd who heard that Elvis was there and ran across the yard to watch. Everyone watched, but Elvis was there for Grandma. He played his classic tunes, he serenaded her, and even did one of his signature moves as he took off his white scarf and put it around her neck.

In the picture I found on Aunt Natalie's old MySpace account, Elvis sings and plays his guitar right in front of Grandma, her hand covering her mouth as she laughs, her family and friends surrounding her, laughing and smiling along with her, taking pictures— all of this to celebrate her. At one point, Grandma wasn't content to stay sitting on her rollator the whole time: she got up and danced. She sang along, she hugged Elvis. And she clapped and cheered when after putting on quite a show, Elvis left the building.

This is joy: something so everlasting and embedded so deep within you that even when you're suffering, you find a way to stand up and dance. It is so strong and durable that it does not weaken in the face of mounting struggles; in fact, it demonstrates its resilience in those moments, rising above and outshining the pain. It is so sure of itself that it does not care what others think, removing all doubt of its existence as you sing along to the music with abandon. Joy is able to say amidst life's hardships, *you are alive and you are loved, so celebrate.*

I wonder if she had a feeling this would be her last birthday, her last celebration, until the victorious celebration of her life and ministry on August 27, 2008, one week after she died. Still, she stood up from that rollator and she danced. Because of how much she loved the music, because of all those people gathered on that summer day to celebrate her, because of joy.

Dear Grandma,

I'm writing to you from Strongsville High School, where I sit in the bleachers watching high school wrestlers in singlets try to pin each other down, anticipating when it will finally be my brother Jake's turn to compete. This is the school you went to, but never graduated from.

I imagine the school doesn't look the same way it did the last time you were here over fifty years ago. Where I see wrestling mats and referees and intense coaches, you saw balloon arches and boys in suits and girls in dresses, excited for what was supposed to be the most magical night of their lives thus far. And I'm sure the gym was filled with music that is much better than what the DJs always played at my school dances in high school. At my prom in 2016, people were grinding, which is supposed to qualify as dancing but really only looks disgusting. At your 1965 prom, you probably saw people actually dancing, classic moves like the mashed potato or the swim. You are so lucky that you went to high school at a time when grinding wasn't a thing.

I sit on the old wooden bleachers, the sound of referees' whistles and people cheering surrounding me; you posed for a picture under a balloon arch with a beehive in your hair and a size four pink dress, your satin-gloved arms wrapped around a boy in a white tux. On the back of that picture you wrote the words "the night Paul was conceived." Nine months later, you'd be holding my dad in your arms for the first time.

For all of the differences between our proms that took place fifty years apart from each other, I think we still had some similar experiences. We both dressed in sixties fashion: you, because you lived the era; me, because I love vintage style and wanted to look as different as possible from the other girls at prom who wore three-hundred dollar (or more) studded, slitted, form-fitting dresses. We both went to prom with a boy in a white tux, and we both left early, although I'm pretty sure it was for different reasons.

My dad's life story began at that high school prom, and now he is a fifty-one year old man sitting in the very gym where that dance was, crossing his arms as he watches his son wrestle, making sure to not miss a single detail so he can talk it over with Jake later. He's a man who misses you so much, whose face lit up when I asked him after the wrestling match if you ever got your GRE, smiling as he said that you did, but you didn't tell anyone all along that you were taking night classes. You told everyone you were teaching piano lessons until one night you came home and announced that you had done it: you got your GRE, and my dad is still proud of you for it.

When I visited Uncle Dan, your "brother Danny" as you always referred to him, in Mississippi,

I asked him how he reacted when he found out that you were pregnant at seventeen years old, if he was shocked or not. He told me that he can only remember feeling happy that he would get to be the first one in your family to receive a high school diploma, considering you would have to drop out. Even though you weren't able to get it then, it's still a huge accomplishment that you were able to get it later on in your life. He also told me that you were really smart in school.

I got home and looked up information about Strongsville High School, and I saw that the building has only been in use since 1968, three years after the night that you went to prom. Everything I imagined was wrong.

But I'm not upset that I got it wrong, because you still walked these halls later on in your life when our church used the Strongsville High School facilities for our Sunday services while our new building was under construction, and I got to walk them alongside you. It was in the school's auditorium that I would see you worship and learn from your example what dedication and faith in Christ looks like. I remember one Christmas Eve, knowing you were sitting behind me, I put my hand up to worship, not knowing what it really meant, just doing it so that I could be like you. I asked you afterwards if you saw me do it, and you told me that you did.

So, I didn't get to see the gym where you had your prom, one of your last memories before your life would be changed forever. And I'm sure the months that followed that night weren't easy for you. But I do get to see the outcome of that night, and it's evident in the picture that sits on our piano: you stand in a Strongsville High School hallway, a case of trophies visible behind you, with three of your four children, their arms around you, making you look really short. You're wearing a leather jacket and a soft grin on your face. The way your eyes shine and crinkle upwards tell me that you were happy, and that things turned out good for you.

Love,

Hanna Grace

Church Bench

We cannot see God. Sometimes that makes it hard to believe in Him, but that fact never seemed to deter Grandma. She was a woman of faith, never missing church, whether it be at Christ Church (our family's church) or The House of the Lord in Akron.

Placing herself perfectly between the southernmost sanctuary door and the front entrance to the church, she could see all. Every person who walked in, stomping the slush off their boots as they walked across the rugs, shaking the hands of the ushers, taking their sunglasses off. Regular attendees, people who knew her, people who didn't, those who may be coming back after a hiatus and feeling uneasy, or those who were attending church for the first time. She sat on that bench, the golden morning light from the tall windows filtering through her blonde hair, making the flyways look like a halo. Grandma could be found on any given week sitting in this very spot, as she looked up at whoever had stopped to talk to her or surveyed the congregants around her.

In fact, besides when she was playing the

piano and the one Sunday that I sat with her during the adult service, I have no memory of my Grandma ever being anywhere else in our church. I can't picture her walking down the hall or coming in from the parking lot. Her spot on the bench became a fixed point, as she was in the church. Concrete, immovable, unchanging. It was the place I'd run to when I heard that Grandma was there, where I'd go to get a piece of Juicy Fruit because she always had some. I never found her alone.

When I ask Jake, who was six years old when she died, what he remembers about Grandma, that's what he says: the Juicy Fruit. Finding Grandma every week sitting on the bench by the front door at church and getting a piece of gum.

Just like Jake, I went to the bench for the Juicy Fruit, but I also remember getting a hug every time. I always thanked her, but looking back, I didn't appreciate it enough. I was used to Grandma and took her consistency and presence for granted. As a child, I still thought of the world as a safe, happy place. Others weren't used to people like her, someone who sat on the bench and stayed there, welcoming all who came in.

We cannot see God. We can worship him, read the Bible, pray to Him, but we cannot see Him. Nothing can change that. For this reason, I've been taught that even though God is invisible, we should be able to see Him through the words, actions, and lives of His followers. From that bench and from every other place she sat and every place she walked, to every person she talked to, by always having a piece of Juicy Fruit and a hug to give, Grandma did exactly this: she showed the world God.

Dear Grandma,

    Most people would rather drive than take the bus, but I love taking the 55 to school for three reasons: I don't have to deal with traffic, I get to read or do homework, and every time I look out the window, there's a good view. I'm not a morning person and have to drag myself out of bed every day, but when I (very rarely) reach my goal and get on the bus at seven a.m., it's all worth it when I get to see the sunrise behind the Cleveland skyline.

    For a long time, I was really into the idea of seeing the mouth of the Cuyahoga River up close. I don't know why I cared about it so much; I guess I just liked the idea of seeing where the river meets the Lake, and how they meet each other. Now, I see where Cuyahoga meets Erie from the Cleveland Memorial Shoreway all the time, so long as I'm sitting on the right side of the bus.

    As I was riding today I took a break from the book I'm reading and struggling to finish amidst all of my homework: A Man Called Ove *by Fredrik Backman. It's a Swedish book but it has gotten really popular worldwide. I think you'd like it because it's a redemption story and has made me cry so far (so you'd definitely be crying), and if you're like me, you love books that make you cry.*

    I looked out the window at the mouth of the Cuyahoga River and the Flats surrounding the area.

The lake looked beautiful to me today, even though I would normally choose a visit to the ocean over one of Ohio's beaches. The water was a lighter shade of blue than normal, with the remaining shards of ice piled up at the water's edge, since the weather has been unseasonably warm the past couple days, considering that it's February and all the snow melted. The river looked brown as usual.

A lot of people tend to love their cities out of pride for their hometown; but for me, it's simple experiences like this that have inspired a love of Cleveland in me, ever since I started going to college at Cleveland State University. Just learning and seeing more, and actually getting to know the city for myself have led to me being able to honestly say that I love Cleveland. Ohio City Burrito (best burritos in the world) and Mitchell's (best ice cream in the world) have also had a lot to do with that. As I looked at the mouth of the Cuyahoga River, I wondered if you loved Cleveland, too.

Whether you loved it or not or even merely liked it, you were a Cleveland girl, born and raised.

You were a first generation midwesterner, your family having migrated from Alabama to Ohio, from the deep south to the North in search of jobs, back when Cleveland was booming.

Your lifetime saw many different Clevelands: you lived on the East side on Broadway Avenue in

31

your early childhood, and later on moved to the West side to Roanoke Avenue. You saw Cleveland in its most prosperous and glowing moments, and you also saw its deterioration, pushing you to move to the suburbs.

There was so much in you, a northern girl with southern blood, traversing East and West, navigating the highs and lows of a city's history— all of this in just one person. You contained multitudes.

I wish I could say the same thing about myself. I've lived in the same place my entire life, never living anywhere besides the suburbs of Cleveland. I went from Brunswick to Lakewood, a West-sider all the way, the East side still completely foreign to me. No one crosses that river easily around here. I moved twenty miles, thirty minutes. That's it. I don't know if I'd be willing to go much further.

Love,

Hanna Grace

A Victorious Celebration of the Life and Ministry of Lucinda F. Kraker

Her funeral was scheduled on the same date as our first day of school. Forever a nerd, I couldn't stand the idea of missing school, even though it was my Grandma's funeral. I wanted her funeral to be changed to a different day, but I wasn't the one in control of these things.

"I read your Grandma's obituary in the newspaper," Mrs. Becks, my fifth grade teacher told me as she walked me down the hallway, as the rest of the class was in music class and I had to leave to go to the funeral.

"Oh." I was staring at the classroom door at the end of the end of the hallway. "You did?"

"It said she was a wonderful musician, that she played piano…"

"Yes, she was the best."

"Oh, honey." Mrs. Becks stopped walking and looked at me. "I know…"

"It's okay," I said. Maybe she thought I would start crying, but I wasn't going to. Not yet.

*

We got to the church and my dad took Jake and me into the sanctuary.

He led us up to her open casket. "They're going to close it up soon."

Death did not become her. She laid in her casket in her purple pantsuit, her face sunken deep into her neck, her mouth frowning, nearing the point of scowling. Her arms lay straight at her side. Everything about her was unnatural.

"Say goodbye to your grandma," Dad directed us. Jake leaned in and kissed her on the cheek, I grabbed her limp hand and stared at her closed eyes.

The last time I had seen her, she was full of life, sitting on the red couch at Uncle Bill's birthday party, the glow of summer surrounding her as she smiled, holding a paper plate.

This corpse in front of me, this cold, rubbery hand that I held, this frowning woman— this was not the Grandma I knew.

*

A packed sanctuary. My Grandma and Grandpa List, my mom's mother and stepfather, sitting in the back, having made the trip from Florida to come to the funeral.

*

The program was ten full pages, 8.5 x 11 inches. Pages of quotes, pictures. No one else has ever gotten a program like that for their funeral at our church.

*

I sat in the second row, the cross before me. Her four children in the front row. Aunt Kelly, one seat away from me to my left, wiping her tears. Uncle Chris sat directly in front of me, hunched over in his black suit, not wearing his usual baseball cap. Aunt Kelly kept reaching over to put her hand on his shoulder.

Amanda sat by herself at the end of the front row, her head in her hands, crying the entire time. I wanted to yell at her, tell her that she shouldn't be sitting in the front row with Grandma's kids, but I just let her sob and didn't say anything.

*

Musicians dressed in black all across the stage, even Aunt Natalie, Grandma's fourth and final child, her first and only daughter, got up there and sang with her eyes closed, her hands gripping the edge of her blazer. She tried to make it through the song, but often stopped singing to just stand there and cry, *when I get where I'm going, there'll be only happy tears.* Bishop Joey and Doc both spoke. A video montage played. I started crying when a picture of me and her floated across the screen. Without me asking, Aunt Kelly handed me a tissue.

We arrived at the part of the funeral where there's an open mic and anyone can come up and say something about the deceased.

My mom walked up to say something, clad in a gray dress and heels. "Paul is a mama's boy and normally that spells T-R-O-U-B-L-E for the daughter-in-law... but it was never like that with Sandie at all..." She couldn't say more than that. At that point, she was crying too much and lost her composure. She handed the mic to the next person and walked back to her seat, lips pursed together but still trembling.

*

The Marinellas sat in the row behind me. Uncle Chris ("Uncle C"), Aunt Tami, David, and Matthew. Recently welcomed into our family after Uncle Bill and Aunt Natalie got into contact with Uncle C, Grandpa Kraker's son from his first marriage, you would have thought they had known Grandma forever by the way Aunt Tami's hand rested on Uncle C's knee, comforting him, by the way they both stared at the floor.

*

I walked around the pond out back afterwards with Caity and two of our friends from church, Garret and Jeremy, two brothers who I would alternate having crushes on throughout my elementary and middle school years. I was still thinking about songs, singing, worshipping.

*

I wish in all of this I would have stopped and

looked at my parents and seen their pain, beyond when my mom stood in front of people at the funeral with a microphone in her hand, and noticed the way they comforted and were there for each other. But I was too much of a child, not as grown up as I thought I was. I just continued life as normal, and I assumed they were doing the same.

I can't remember anything else about her funeral and besides, why would I want to? Out of all the memories, those are not the ones I want to keep, but they are the freshest. Even as I write this, drawing out of my mind what I can remember of this day, I'm filled with the sounds of hallelujah. The song "Hallelujah what a Savior" by Tommy Walker plays in iTunes as I type.

That's what I want to remember, what I *will* remember: the hallelujahs. A triumphant life. A victorious celebration.

*

My friend Sarah was told by her mom to leave me alone as Grandma's casket was being lowered into the ground. The members of our family threw dirt into her grave under the shade of the cemetery trees, the leaves their fullest green.

Dear Grandma,

Fifty-two years ago today, you became a mother at seventeen. You had already become a wife, having married Paul Jackson, your high school sweetheart and prom date, a couple months prior. He stood next to you at Metro Hospital as you gave birth to your first son, my dad, Paul Fitzpatrick Jackson. Only one-third of his name is still the same.

That idea that you were seventeen and already a wife and mother, is unfathomable to me at nineteen. When I was seventeen, I was finishing my senior year, dating my first boyfriend, thinking of graduation and the looming AP exams on the horizon. That boyfriend didn't last; in fact, today as I was shopping for my dad's present at JC Penney the mall, I saw his mom from a distance and I had a moment of immaturity, as I promptly turned around and power-walked out of the store. I know it's bad and that I need to learn that you can't always avoid awkward situations, but what's done is done and I avoided it this time.

After finding my dad a present at a different store, I drove to church to see him. I sat with him in his office as he scrolled through all of the birthday wishes people had posted on his Facebook wall. I think he thinks a lot about you on his birthday, at least more than other days. He clicked on a picture of you that Aunt Natalie had posted. The bottom of the polaroid dated the picture at September 1973. You were twenty-five years old, wearing a purple shirt, and you smiled with your teeth. You leaned on the table, a half-eaten birthday cake in front of you, signifying, along with date, that you had just been celebrating Uncle Chris's first birthday. My dad swiveled the mouse around your face, and told me that I look so much like you as he leaned back in his office chair, eating his new creation, cookie dough sandwiched between two cookies (the materials for this sandwich were my birthday present to him). I can see the resemblance, but not as much as he does.

I'll be twenty in April and while it feels like its only significance is that it's one year away from turning twenty-one, to be honest, it makes me a little nervous. I find it hard to believe that I'm about to reach the "twenties" and that I'll be in the decade when people establish a career, get married, start a family, and have their lives figured out— at least that's what I've heard and what the movies and Instagram make the twenties seem like. I oftentimes have to remind myself that I'm an adult, because most of the time I don't feel like one. When you turned twenty, you were seven months pregnant with Uncle Bill.

My dad can't believe that he's fifty-two, and neither can my Uncle Bill and Aunt Natalie who came out to dinner with us tonight. They said that fifty-two sounds so old, that you're the one who should be fifty-two and not my dad. They just can't believe how fast time goes.

    I'm not saying my life is so much better than yours was when you were my age. Just that it's different.

Love,

Hanna Grace

Nondenominational

Some of my friends are Catholic, others Methodist, Lutheran, Baptist, or nothing at all. I was something a little different and a lot less pronounceable: nondenominational. As we grew up, I began to see the differences in our respective churches. While they thought of things to give up for Lent, got confirmed, sang hymns in pews every week, got baptized as babies, I had a completely different church experience.

I went to Christ Church, where I've gone my entire life and where I still go today. It's a church where the kids dance to worship songs and watch skits for their lessons, people of all ages get baptized either in the tub onstage or the pond out back, and my dad, as the creative arts pastor, finds ways to put rock songs like "Free Bird" into Sunday's set list because they relate to the sermon. Our church has been led by Doctor Dave Collings, who everyone calls "Doc" for short, for our over thirty-five years. On any given week, he can be seen arriving at church in his pickup truck, wearing a leather jacket and cowboy boots.

Every Sunday the doors open, the band plays, and Doc preaches, hoping to reach the free birds who feel like they can't change and that there's no hope for them, and show them that there's a way.

The way our church operates is with no allegiance or ties to any denomination— that's one way to be nondenominational. We just follow the Bible. And even though we're considered "nondenominational", we still have our way of doing things. Whenever I visit another church, it always feels a little foreign to me.

My Grandma was nondenominational, but in an entirely different way.

One time at a family party Grandma passed out yellow folders to everyone. Inside the folder, she had put pages of a story called "Cindy Lu" in plastic sleeves.

I looked at the title. "Who's Cindy Lu?" I asked my dad.

"It's your grandma," he replied, pointing to her.

"Huh?" My mouth hung open in confusion. I always thought that Sandie was her first name.

"Her real name is Lucinda. Cindy Lu was her nickname as a kid, and somewhere along the way, no one really knows why, that was turned into Sandie," he explained, laughing at that last part.

"Ohhh," I replied, the lightbulb going off.

Within this yellow folder, she recorded the beginning of a story which she planned on finishing, but never did. In this first and final installment, she wrote about her childhood when she lived on the East side of Cleveland and began her journey in her Christian faith.

Her first encounters with church were going to Catholic mass with her aunt and uncle when she was in kindergarten: *"They would walk down the Broadway Ave, to the big Catholic Church and Cindy Lu just loved it, because she wanted all of God!"* This was something she decided to do on her own, the only member of her household to do this. Every Sunday she'd wake up on her own, get ready, and walk with her cousins to church. A five-year old.

This didn't last very long, because her family was from Alabama, which was right in the middle of the largely-protestant "Bible Belt" part of America, so they made her stop going to the Catholic church. But she wouldn't give church up: *"So, since Cindy Lu kept begging to go to church, her mom had no choice but to take her and her brothers to church! So they went the other way down Broadway Ave to the big Methodist Church, and again she loved the Sunday School Class!"* It was like going to church was what she was meant to do.

She heard the call, and she answered.

Grandma raised her kids in a local Baptist

church, and it was the kind of Baptist that was very "fundamental" with all of its rigid rules, as described by my dad.

My dad, a self-proclaimed hellion, has never done well submitting to authority. As a kid, he (accidentally) set his dining room on fire, peed on the pillow of Grandma's soon-to-be husband after he had chastised my dad for something that he can't even remember anymore. He pushed Uncle Chris, who was probably five years old at this time, out of the house naked and locked the doors. In high school in cahoots with his best friend, Jim, he flushed fireworks down the toilets at school and smeared crisco on the hallway floors so that when the bell rang, all of the students slipped and fell as they exited the classrooms. So, it makes a lot of sense that my dad didn't do too well in a strict church.

One time, the youth pastor tried to get my dad in trouble.

"You know," he told my grandma in an insinuating tone after service. "Your son knows all of the rock songs and can play them on his guitar."

This was the type of church where secular music, especially rock and roll, was regarded as the devil's music.

"I know," Grandma replied, so sweetly and yet defiantly. "He's so talented." She didn't conform to their fundamental mindset, because little did they

44

know that she had her own rock music records at home and could play them, too.

My dad started taking classes at Cuyahoga County Community College, which is better known as Tri-C, but he soon took a semester off after being put on academic probation because he only applied himself in his music classes and didn't really care about the others. During that time he decided to go to college to become a pastor when he was twenty-one years old. He went to Southeastern College in Lakeland, Florida, a small Christian school in the Assemblies of God tradition.

Once again, in a fundamental religious setting, my dad struggled with authority. It was at this college that he met my mom, who was studying to become a teacher, when she was working in the cafeteria and took his tomatoes from his hamburger when he didn't want them. Now, when we visit Florida and drive by the campus, he'll point out where the trailers used to be, the ones he was "banished" to because he got put on probation and kicked out of the dorms.

After they graduated and got married, my dad was pastoring a church in downtown Lakeland called Grace Church as part of the Calvary Chapel Evangelical Movement. My Uncle Bill and Aunt Liz had even moved down from Missouri, where Uncle Bill went to college at Evangel University, to join

45

them.

But then my Grandma started telling them about a church she had started going to in Strongsville called Christ Church. She talked about how she absolutely loved it and how she had told the pastor, Doc, all about her son Paul who was a pastor down in Florida.

They asked my dad to take a position at Christ Church and move back to Ohio. He spent an entire day at Clearwater Beach, sitting on the sand and staring at the waves. The same beach he had proposed to my mom on, the same beach he'd be praying for my life on after my mom got pregnant with me. He prayed, and he made his decision.

He started working at Christ Church as the discipleship pastor in 1996 and would go onto become the creative arts pastor later on. Soon thereafter I was born and was raised in Christ Church. I've spent so much time there over the years that I consider it my second home.

I would dance in the pews with my cousins as the band played. I would sit in the back with Grandma, or at the piano with her, seeing the red marks she had left on the keys from her manicures.

I would see my Grandma sitting in the front row, putting her hand up.

When we built our new building in Columbia Station because our church was getting too big for the

Strongsville building, I would see her on the bench. Always.

Grandma's nondenominational-ism not only successfully and peacefully navigated the Catholic-Protestant division and even the divisions within protestantism: it also maneuvered the racial divisions that often exist in Christianity. While there are diverse churches out there, it's just a fact that churches tend to be predominantly white or predominantly black. Grandma didn't care.

When she wasn't at Christ Church, she was at the House of the Lord in Akron, a majority African American church, where her faith continued to grow and where she developed many close friendships. The styles of those two churches were very different, but she fit right in at either place.

Grandma had an immense appreciation for the African American church culture. She loved the expressive atmosphere during worship and how the congregants frequently talk back to the preacher. Her brother Paul did in-depth, years-long research on their family tree, going all the way back to the 14th century in Scotland. What he found out was that he and his siblings were 16% African American. Though this is a pretty small percentage, Grandma was thrilled when she found out and so proud that she had African American ancestors on both sides of her family tree—one side of the family coming from Alabama sharecroppers, the other side coming from Eastern Kentucky.

On April 20, 2008, four days after my tenth birthday— double digits!— Grandma took me to church with her. Normally, trips to the House of the Lord were a family affair, but as part of her birthday gift to me, it was just going to be her and me this time.

Her white explorer took us down 71, down Route 18 through Medina and past Swenson's, then to 77 to Akron. It's a little bit of a hike to get there, but it's worth it.

The programs were purple. The color of royalty, the color of the robes the mobs put on Jesus as he was flogged after being sentenced to crucifixion. Grandma's and my favorite color. Across the top, above the images of trumpets blasting, were the words "The Year of the Call". Looking back, those words are too true: 2008 really was the year of the call for Grandma— the year that she was called home. We all stood as Bishop Joey walked in, the leader of the growing congregation and close friend of my Grandma.

The music and the sermon went on for about two hours, but to me it felt endless. As a ten year old, the "adult" service as I viewed it, was usually boring to me no matter if I was at my own church listening to Doc or at another church. I just found it hard to pay attention.

The service was all-around very different from Christ Church. Besides being twice the length, the worship was a lot more energetic and alive, as a lot of the people in the audience would dance and jump, while some even brought their own tambourines. Bishop Joey would sometimes start singing in the middle of his sermon.

Afterwards, I met a lot of people. I shook their hands and then sat there quietly as my Grandma talked to them about adult things. Before we left, someone took our picture.

She smiles a soft smile, I lean my head on her shoulder and smile with my teeth. We both fix our brown eyes on the camera. It came out black-and-white and was stuck on Grandma's fridge. I saw it there when we were going through her house after she died. I saw it there, and I never grabbed it.

Today, this yellow folder containing Cindy Lu's story sits in the bottom drawer of my dresser. I reread it every year on June 25th and August 20th, feeling evermore grateful that I get to learn part of her life story in her own words, rather than hear the stories passed down through other sources.

As I flip the laminated pages, skim the pages and see some words in all caps, some sentences followed by multiple exclamation marks, I realize that people find different ways to God. I'm not one for mass, for standing and kneeling over and over again, or Ash Wednesday and other traditions like that. But my friends experience God in that way.

In all our different ways, we find Him. Some get baptized as babies, the priest pouring water over their head. Some, like me, give their lives to God and then get baptized as an outward symbol of that. Others go through life battered and worn, find their way, and then are dunked under the water, coming back up with fists pumping and cheers from the crowd, welcomed into their new life. Some raise their hands and dance when they worship, some stand still and soak it all in, worshiping in their hearts.

We go through life, we rejoice, we hurt, we hear His voice, we hear the call, and we answer. We run our races fixing our eyes on the same God.

Grandma found Him everywhere, in every way, from the time she was five years old and onward: *"Cindy had no way of knowing then, but the Lord had created her, chosen her, and given her a hunger and thirst for the Lord, to last a lifetime! How blessed she was!"* I reread Grandma's words and I get to take a trip to her childhood in Cleveland. I get to see the beginning of her Christian journey unfold, and I'm reminded that faith is a gift, and that being blessed is not about what you can get from God, but just simply knowing Him and knowing that you're His.

I think about the way her walk with God continued beyond the time of Cindy Lu, and I see that Grandma didn't choose just one denomination, one church. She chose God, and went wherever He was. Hands raised, heart full, hunger and thirst quenched, unquenchable. Ever-searching, she found Him.

Dear Grandma,

I can't believe you had the chance to see him, and you didn't go. You had the tickets in your hand, and you gave them away. Your reason was pretty valid— you were too pregnant— but Uncle Bill still wishes you would have stuck it out and gone anyways, so that he could say he went to an Elvis concert, even if he was only there via your womb.

The Elvis room at the Rock and Roll Hall of Fame in downtown Cleveland is less of a room and more a shrine. People fall silent when they walk into that space. His gold suit stands in a case and one of his motor cars is roped off for visitors to look at but not touch; but besides that, the main focus of his exhibit is the documentary that plays on a giant screen on one wall, showing clips of his concerts and various musicians talking about how influential he was. I sat on the benches in front of the screen and watched the entire thing, as people filled up the rest of the bench space and stood on the sides. People ceased their meandering through the exhibits, and stood fixated in front of the King.

The concert clips were from his Hawaii Elvis days. He's wearing a white body suit and leis around his neck, not chubby Elvis, but Elvis with shaggy hair. He could still perform, though. I got chills even though the recordings are over forty years old. The goosebumps ran all up my arms mainly during

"Burning Love" as the background singers joined in during the chorus. I didn't even feel annoyed that he had to read the lyrics off a piece of paper in his hand, and even then he got the words wrong. If he was that amazing while visibly strung out on drugs and on video, I can't imagine what he would have been like in person.

The movie also went into detail about his early career and movies and how all those young girls went crazy over him because he was such a heartthrob. I know for you that it wasn't just about his looks or his dance moves. For you, it was about the music, and everything else about him was just a bonus. When the Elvis impersonator performed at your sixtieth birthday party, you stood away from your rollator and danced like it was Elvis himself.

After the Elvis movie was over, I went to the Beatles exhibit and watched the documentary playing there. In the Beatles vs. Elvis debate, I'm sorry, but I definitely sway towards the Beatles. My dad said you wouldn't listen to the Beatles because you thought Elvis was the best and didn't like that people were saying that they were better than him. I'm sure we would have had some fun conversations about that, although I guess without Elvis, we wouldn't have the Beatles. So maybe you would've won the debate.

I'm still an Elvis fan though. I've always been one of those people who loves dancing in their bedroom, who when the door is closed and the music is blasting, will suddenly be filled with the notion that my room is Madison Square Garden, and that I am the performer that everyone is there to see. One time I was listening to "Burning Love", in my room and I shouted and pointed up, "Grandma, this is for you!" and proceeded to jump around, sometimes on the bed, sometimes while playing air guitar. I was probably eleven at the time.

In our family we're all Elvis fans, if not because of the music, always because of you. Aunt Natalie got married to her fiancé, my soon-to-be Uncle Joe, at Graceland. I remember that January morning in Memphis, rainy and cold, but not as cold as Ohio. Down a cobblestone path that led to a little cottage behind the chapel, the wedding party was getting ready. Emily, Caity, Hannah Mae (Uncle Joe's daughter from a previous marriage) and myself were the flower girls. I was five years old at the time, a kindergartner. I don't remember what you were doing. Probably crying, disposable camera in hand. At least that's what you're doing in the pictures from my parents' wedding. I got my hair curled, afraid of getting burned and that the hairspray would sting my eyes, and that's about all I can remember from that cottage. And I also remember that I felt like a princess, mostly because the only other times I had heard of cottages were in fairy tales.

I bet you laughed, through more tears, as us four flower girls ran down the aisle. We must have all gotten nervous when we saw the crowd of people looking at us. When Emily, our line leader, ran, we all followed suit.

We toured Graceland afterwards, and I'm sure that if it was your first time there, you were going crazy. All I can remember is the orange couches and my brother screaming, throwing a tantrum. He was two years old, and my dad had to take him outside to calm him down. Caity swears that she saw swimming trunks floating around in the guitar-shaped pool, but I cannot verify that. All I remember of the reception is hiding underneath a table with the cousins, peeking out every once in a while, bored by all the fanciness around us.

Aunt Natalie named her first son Presley, whom she was three months pregnant with at the time of the wedding.

When we want to pay tribute to you, we eat chocolate, we go to Master Pizza, and we listen to Elvis.

To all of us, you and Elvis are inextricably linked.
Love,
Hanna Grace

The Phone Company

We know when things are bad for us, and yet we still do it.

Grandma worked almost all the way up until her death. When I was a kid, I referred to her job as "the phone company", but my dad recently cleared this up and said that she worked for customer service at AT&T, answering calls and helping people solve their problems.

"She was probably the best at that job," Dad said as we drove home from one of Jake's wrestling matches. "You would have been lucky to call and get to have her handle your problems. Most people you talk to are morons, but she was always so nice and encouraging."

It seems like she was happy there. I remember a picture of her with Slider, the Indians' Mascot, who had come to visit her office that day.

He also said that she'd have to take breaks as she walked into work, because she'd be so out of breath. Once she'd get inside, she'd get her work done, her headset on, ready to take the next caller.

She'd put in her hours, and then she'd leave and walk out, possibly taking more breaks on her way to the parking lot. She'd get in her car, and on her way home, she'd oftentimes go through the drive thru at Burger King.

Dear Grandma,

Based on what people have told me and even based on what you've given me, I know that you were good with words. That's one of the things that people remember the most about you: the writing. The letters, the notes. You were encouraging and so caring through your words, and if my birthday cards from you are any indication, these notes often weren't very long. You found a way to say what matters without having to ramble to prove your point. I tend to ramble pretty much every time I open my mouth, but I'm going to try to do adopt your style as I write to you because it seemed to be very effective. We'll see how it goes.

Firstly, I've been thinking that you give us all a reason to write, whether that be songs, Facebook posts, or books. Ten years later, people are still writing about you. You inspire people.

Second, I found one of your Bibles tonight, sitting on the bottom shelf of my mom's glass table that she puts plants on. The inside cover said that it was given to you by my dad on Christmas day of 1986. The pages crinkled as I flipped them, exploring your highlighting throughout, comparing it to the annotations in mine. Different verses and words have stuck out to us individually and you preferred to read with colored highlighters while I use multicolored pens, but it's obvious that we share a love of the book of Romans.

And lastly, to really adopt your style, I'm going to end on this: I love you and I'm proud of you.

I love you because you're my Grandma. Because you were so kind and thoughtful, you were really good at listening and you genuinely cared about everyone. Because you wrote verses and quotes from sermons all over the inside cover of your Bibles, such as Matthew 11:28: "Come to me all who are weary and heavy laden and I will give you rest." Because even though you're not on Earth anymore, you're still a mentor to me in the form of worn-out Bibles, handwritten quotes, and colorful highlighting, inspiring me to love and follow Jesus better.

One of my favorite childhood books, Walk Two Moons *by Sharon Creech, is titled after the mantra "Don't judge a man until you walk two moons in his moccasins." I'm proud of you because you walked some pretty tough moons in some hard-worn moccasins that would not have been sensible footwear in the Cleveland winter. I'm proud of you because strangers probably judged you harshly, never thinking about those moons you walked, concluding that all there was to know about you was your size; but you constantly showed grace, never judging them back.*

I tried to write short, sweet, and concise, but I guess that's your style and not mine. And I'm okay with that, because I like that we're different.
Love,
Hanna Grace

5035 Center Road

Mr. Wheeler wasn't a good neighbor. Grumpy
all the time, he didn't even try to pretend to care about
his neighbors and was openly unpleasant all the time.
His driveway lining up right next to Grandma's, he'd
plow snow without considering that it piled up on her
side. After she died, we discovered that he was
trapping groundhogs and keeping them in her shed.
That shed, once Aunt Natalie's playhouse, housed
groundhogs even in her childhood. One time when she
was a little girl (or so she claims), Aunt Natalie
opened the door to her house only to find herself face-
to-face with one. The way she tells it, she screamed
and it chased her across the yard to the house, until she
threw open the back door and fell down the basement
stairs because she was running so fast.

When Grandma lived alone and never went
upstairs, my mom discovered that there was a squirrel
living in Aunt Natalie's old room, having gotten in
through the open window, and that that was the source
of the scratching, scuffling noise that Grandma had
been hearing.

The squirrel's room was covered in Aunt Natalie's old posters of Bob Marley and dancers' masks, the closet stuffed with her old clothes. Aunt Natalie had gotten that room after my dad moved to Florida for college. When it was his bedroom, he was tormented by the ghost of an old lady, probably the woman who killed herself in the house before my family lived there. Every night he'd close the closet door, but when he'd wake up the next morning, it would be open. He started stuffing clothes into the cracks so there was no possible way it could open on its own, only for it to be wide open come morning. He decided that it was the old lady and came to peace with it.

Move down the hall, past the bathroom that never worked in my lifetime, the waterless toilet with chipped paint always giving me the creeps, and enter Uncle Chris's room. When my parents moved back from Florida and didn't have a house yet, it became their room. It's the same room I watched Willy Wonka and the Chocolate Factory with my step-cousin Hannah Mae and Uncle Joe at three in the morning, and I couldn't decide if I was more afraid of the Oompa Loompas or Erik Von Newtonburg, the ghost who haunted this room. My dad told me that Erik Von Newtonburg was the man who built Grandma's Cape Cod style home (he was really ahead of his time) back in the seventeen-hundreds, but tragically met his end when he was riding his horse in the backyard and a tree branch fell and knocked his head off. When my dad told me that story, I was so scared that I slept on my brother's bedroom floor that night, hoping he could protect me, even though he was terrified himself and had cried as he listened to our dad.

The un-haunted bedroom in the middle was my sister Amanda's room when she lived there, her Pocahontas poster still on the wall. In the room sat the black day bed Amanda and I shared one Christmas Eve, when we all used to sleepover at Grandma's and open presents together the next morning. But then our family got too big and we stopped that tradition. Even that night, before I had heard any of the ghost stories, I was too scared to sleep. The branches of the pine trees outside were silhouetted by the streetlights, creating long, spindly shadows across the walls. Amanda slept soundly next to me while I stared at the ceiling, convinced that the nighttime had conspired with the wind to make this house as creepy as possible, knowing I would be sleeping there.

Those trees would be freaking me out again in the aftermath of Grandma's death and Hurricane Ike, as my mom and I were at the uninhabited house alone. The high winds and torrential rain had traveled all the way from Florida to Ohio, instilling us with the hope that school might be canceled. I imagined that the house was shaking under the rain, the wind waking the ghosts that I was sure were lurking behind me. My mom wanted to get some work done at the house, but I couldn't wait to leave.

A portrait of Jesus hung at the top of the stairs, the same stairs that the family would sit on every Christmas morning to take a picture before coming down to see our presents around the tree. He stares upwards, his long hair swept over one shoulder, the entire painting comprised of shades of gold and green.

At the foot of the stairs, take a right to see Grandma's bedroom, her Hampton Inn mattresses like massive, dense pillows, recently given to her as birthday present from her kids. In the middle of the wooden headboard sat the pillow with all of her grandkids painted handprints on display. We gave her this pillow on her sixtieth birthday, and two months later, she'd be buried with it. On her nightstand, all of her journals and her Bibles, always full of annotations in the margins and highlights throughout. The room was always dim, the lights never on, the massive wooden armoire and dresser seeming to cloud the room and darken it further.

Go to the adjacent room which I called the music room, which contained two, nonfunctioning organs and Grandpa's old army swords and guns from Vietnam inside a locked, wooden case, which mesmerized every kid who went in there. Caity and I would share the bench at one of the organs, which we called our prayer machine. We'd flip up all the blue switches to activate it. Folding our hands, we'd close our eyes and pray silently to ourselves. After we had both said *amen,* we'd flip all of the switches back, our prayer machine deactivated and back to its ordinary self. The organ rested against the closet door, the same one Uncle Chris had once hid inside when the room was Aunt Natalie's, jumping out when she walked in and scaring her so much that she peed her pants.

The downstairs bathroom had a green bathtub and a blurry window. When we were little, all of the girl cousins would go to the bathroom together. We weren't self-conscious about our bodies yet. We'd sit in there, opening the drawers that smelled like baby powder and examining Grandma's eyelash curler and tweezers, doing nothing with them because we didn't know what they were, and we'd sing Hannah Montana or other Disney songs.

Walk back down the hallway and arrive in the kitchen. Against one wall was a desk, holding up her old green mac monitor that my dad, always an Apple enthusiast had set up for her. She used it to type "Cindy Lu", that story about her childhood that she printed out for all of her family to read.

A giant window against the opposite wall

faced the backyard, where you could see grandkids playing kickball or baseball with Uncle Chris, who was a talented player when he was young, his old home plate still nailed into the ground. On that windowsill stood a pink angel figurine that I took with me after she died. The table always had a bowl of chips on it, a box of cookies, bottles of pop. Above the stove where Grandma could often be found making the goopiest, best-tasting scrambled eggs that no one can replicate, was a mark in the brick wall. Legend has it that it was a bullet mark left by the woman that lived there before my family when she committed suicide.

Go through the archway into the living room. Her old piano was given to Caity as a birthday present, as she was our generation's piano player. In its place was a new, electronic piano that she could record herself on. That piano now sits at Uncle Chris's house and I can picture him sitting at it, listening to her play even though she's not physically there. Also in the room were two brown leather couches, a worn patch expanding more and more on one cushion in particular, the spot she sat on for hours each day as she watched TV.

The basement is all that's left on the inside of the house, comprised of unfinished stairs leading to a concrete floor covered by boxes of memories, a washer and dryer tucked into one corner. When the basement wasn't flooded from the malfunctioning sump pump hole in the floor, my brother would go stare into it, scared that demons would crawl out of there at any second. After she died and the whole family would go to clean the house, I'd go in the basement with Caity and rifle through all of the boxes. Aunt Natalie always had a lot of boyfriends growing up, and we'd look through the pictures of them, laughing at them in their 90s fashion, and choose the ones we thought were the cutest and would want to be our boyfriends.

Go out the back door, and walk down the deck to the yard, the deck she loved sitting on in the summer.

Underneath the deck lay a long ladder, which Uncle Chris would prop against his window when he wanted to sneak out. Between two trees on the side of the house was the horse that Uncle Bill made out of the lumber from a tree he cut down in the yard. We all loved it, through Emily and Caity were the horseback riders for real. The horse went through a series of names, and the only ones I can remember were Betsy and Buttercup, the latter the one that ended up sticking. In that yard, we'd play and play, creating worlds and fighting each other, all of us wanting to be the one on Buttercup, or just talking to each other as we climbed trees. We did all this without venturing too close to the road, as Center Road was the busiest road in Brunswick, though Grandma's house was past the commercial part of it.

We'd stop playing at once when we heard the piano coming from the house.

We'd run back in, and join the crowd of adults surrounding her. All the grandkids would yell, *play the Boogie Woogie!* And she'd smile and nod, able to look around at us as her manicured fingers traveling up and down the keys, her two hands doing completely different things.

Everything happened at that house. It was the headquarters of our family. When my family was there, I wasn't afraid of the ghosts or the sump pump or the bullet hole above the stove.

But that house was also where nothing happened. When there wasn't a family party, it was just Grandma. Grandpa Kraker was there until he died of cancer in November 1998, a couple months after I was born, and I remember Aunt Natalie still living there when I was little, but that wasn't for very long.

I think of the house, and I think of how lonely it must have been. As her health declined, she couldn't maintain it anymore and everything got dusty, As sunlight filtered in through the un-curtained windows, the dust was visible in the beams, tiny particles floating in the light. It was too hard for her to walk up the stairs, so she couldn't take care of the squirrel situation.

Our family was what brought life to it. When we were gone, all that was left was my Grandma and the ghosts. And sometimes the squirrel.

And now it sits, an empty shell on Center Road as cars zip by it at fifty miles an hour. It's repainted, updated on the inside. But it's empty.

On Sundays, whenever I would wake up early enough, I would ride to church with my dad. He would always honk or wail "Mama" dramatically as we passed the house, or mention how he wished he would have stopped by more when he had the chance. I would crane my neck, trying to see if Buttercup the horse was still there. I never could find it though, because my dad drove fast and soon the house would be out of sight.

Vacation

All she ever wanted, she found in Jamaica. She loved it so much because she had never traveled before, my dad told me.

Growing up, I would hear Aunt Natalie or Grandma mention Jamaica. I always thought it had something to do with the Bob Marley poster on Aunt Natalie's closet door in her old bedroom at Grandma's house. I later found out that that's where Grandma and Aunt Natalie went on vacation together and had the time of their lives.

In our den there's a glass table that holds plants on the top shelf, and an assortment of CDs and books on the bottom shelf. Among these books are two of Grandma's journals that she took with her on four of her trips to Jamaica with Aunt Natalie.

Trip one: "Heavenly!! Tropical Paradise!"

Trip two: "seven glorious days!!!"

Trip three: "I'm going to have fun, I can feel it!!"

Trip four: "each time gets better and better!"

Four trips from 1998-2000. I was shocked to

realize that they traveled there that much. I was even more shocked when I texted Aunt Natalie and she told me that they actually went eleven times in total. I would love to be able to read the other seven accounts of their tropical escapades. They were able to go so much because Aunt Natalie was a travel agent during those years and got a lot of good deals. One time at the airport, their flight was overbooked so they volunteered to wait for the next one, and as a reward for doing that, they were given five hundred dollars in travel credit, each. Grandma, in her journal, wrote, "for our next flight to Jamaica!!", without a second thought. They already knew that they'd be going there again.

Grandma hadn't had many opportunities to travel in her life, the many trips to Alabama to visit family notwithstanding. There's a black and white picture of her on top of the Empire State Building when she was a teenager, a trip she got to take with a friend. I wonder if she dreamed of traveling more, since traveller's blood seems to run in our family; but, she became a mom and lived many years in poverty, so any dreams she might have had to explore the world got put on hold. When her kids were older, they took two family vacations, one to Washington D.C. and another to Disney World. But it's "no problem mon" (as she wrote in her journal with a smiley face after having some difficulties in the airport and finally arriving in Jamaica), because in the last ten years of her life, she got to travel *a lot* to a place that she absolutely loved.

Vacation has a way of emboldening people. For many people, that reason is alcohol; but for others, I think it's the anonymity, the idea that these other vacationers don't know you, that you'll most likely never see them again, and whatever happens, you're boarding a flight home in a couple days, so what's the harm in being bold and doing something a little crazy, something you'd never do at home?

From what I gathered from the journals, Aunt Natalie didn't act any differently than she did at home. She always had a lot of boyfriends in Cleveland, so her flirting, dancing, and going on dates with guys in Jamaica was no surprise. But *Grandma.* She was bold. Upon arrival in Jamaica, she wrote the words, "We're here! FINALLY! And going to live it up and enjoy ourselves!" And live it up she did.

I'm reading the journals, my mouth hanging wide open in surprise when my mom knocks on my door to let me know that we're leaving soon to go to dinner for my dad's 53rd birthday.

"Mom!" I hold the journal up to show her what I'm referring to. "Did you know about all of this? Grandma flirted with all these guys in Jamaica and even *kissed* one of them!"

"Oh, yeah," she nods. "I remember hearing

that those Jamaica trips got pretty crazy."

I realize that dancing and going on dates with some guys on the island, sharing one kiss with one of them, is pretty tame behavior. But it's shocking stuff when it's your grandma in this scenario.

Side note: this all happened on the trips *after* Grandpa died in 1998. Grandma wasn't like that, and as reality slowly settled back into place on their flight home, she reflected on the men she met and wrote that she probably is, and always will be, a "one-man woman". Grandpa Kraker was it for her.

They stayed at the Beaches Negril Resort. Grandma writes of lounging on their four-poster bed in their room, reading by the beach during the day while Aunt Natalie was taking dance and snorkeling lessons, or hung out with one of the guys that she met. Every night Grandma went to the piano bar and disco, listened to the music and danced, and even held hands with a thirty-two year old Jamaican man that she met on the resort. No schedule, no excursions planned, just taking each day as it came and loving every second.

Something that I've learned about Grandma from these journals is that she was so honest. I won't divulge anymore specifics than I already have since it is her personal journal and I can't exactly ask her permission to share what she wrote, but what I can say is that she definitely put it all there on the page.

Grandma chronicled every part of their vacation, not just the shining moments. She told it like it was, and in my eyes, that's another kind of boldness.

Aunt Natalie and Grandma did take one vacation that wasn't to Jamaica. Eleven out of twelve vacations still shows some crazy dedication to a place, though. One time, they decided to change it up and go on a Royal Caribbean cruise to Key West and the Bahamas. I remember seeing pictures from that vacation, mainly of their room. Grandma was so excited that their cabin had a porthole.

I read Grandma's accounts of her time in Jamaica, as crazy as they were, and I remember those pictures she took on her cruise, and I have one wish for all of us: may we make how we feel and act on vacation a part of our reality.

May we all jump headfirst into the opportunities we're given, fully immersing ourselves into the joy of the present, not sitting there wishing it had come sooner, only grateful that at this moment, you had a boarding pass and you got to get on a plane and go. May we seize the goodness that is all around us, wringing it until it's dry, experiencing it to the full, and one day come back, realizing that there is always more: more joy to be felt, more fun to be had, more life to be lived. May we be bold, because even though it's difficult and frightening, we should do what makes us happy without caring about what other people think.

May we love that four-poster bed, may we walk on the beach, and when the music comes on, may we dance with strangers and maybe even let them hold our hands. May we write in all caps with several exclamation points, may we indulge our excitement and let it out, loving every little detail. May we love that porthole in our room, finding great joy in the simplest of things. May we gaze out of it, scooting over so that we can all look out together, watching the sun set on the infinite sea, opening it up and taking in the sound of the waves and the parties all around us.

And most importantly, may the best part of all this be that we get to do theses things with people we love. May we love each other and love living this life together, wherever we're at.

Dear Grandma,

Can I just take a second to be angry?

I'm angry that chocolate makes you fat, and that some certain people can be very rude, and that it would be rude of me to name them even though I really want to right now. I'm angry that I can only parallel park so long as there's no traffic around and I can take all the time I need to get it right. I'm angry that I prayed but I still feel angry, that it's all bubbling to the surface. I'm angry that I'm shopping for a birthday present at an antique shop for my friend who shall not be named, who hasn't remembered my birthday for the past three years, but has sent at least five text messages reminding me that her birthday is coming up, as if I'm the friend who forgets.

Fast forward to my-friend-who-shall-not-be-named's birthday party the next day, and I'm not angry. I'm having fun, dancing at a dingy sports bar with my other friend Kayla, who paid me five dollars to drive down to Akron for the second installment of our-friend-who-shall-not-be-named's birthday party (we had already gone to her house in Brunswick for dinner and cake) so she wouldn't be alone. I get angry again when we walk back to the front of the bar where everyone was sitting, only to find that they had all left without telling us. After the party as I'm driving home, I'm angry that it's raining. That construction is everywhere, and I can't find the way to merge onto I-77 because Siri is a computer and yet she's still an idiot and all I see can see through my moving windshield wipers are orange cones and the red Firestone sign in the distance.

I finally made it home though. And sorry that was way more than a second. I was having a moment.

I get so embarrassed about feeling angry. It's something I want to hide, bottle up for as long as I can, until it gets to the point that I'm yelling at my phone. And then I get angry that I let myself get angry, that I admitted that I was feeling this way. Even when this anger only comes up in bursts, lasts for five minutes and then subsides, and even when I'm usually not upset about most of these things, I still hate feeling angry. But you make me feel better about it, because I've heard that you got angry quite a bit. I never saw it for myself and find it hard to believe, but my dad says that you had an angry streak, especially when you were younger.

My dad tells stories of yanked hair, of you screaming at him as he crawled underneath the tables at the donut shop in Strongsville where you were working at the time, that you freaked out every time your kids talked about you in the third person, saying something like "she's acting crazy today" under their breath when you were in the same room as them. When a lady at our church complained about Dad, the way he recalls it, you "blasted" her right there in the church hallway, telling her that whether he was your son or not, no one disrespects a pastor. And I'm sure that rude people, friends forgetting about you, and feeling lost and confused would make you feel angry, too.

But you weren't an angry person— any one who knew you knows that. And it seems like you got better at managing your anger as life went on. But you make me feel a little better, because even someone like you, who I thought was an angel, got mad too.

It's okay to get angry. It's natural and I shouldn't let my feelings bottle up all the time. I have to remember that. I also have to remember to not get lost in that feeling, and to look around and see all of the reasons that I have to not be angry.

Love,

Hanna Grace

Visit #5

Thank God I wrote this one down. Otherwise, it would have been left out, because I forgot about it.

A girl's night out, we went to the Cavs game. My Grandma, my mom, Aunt Liz, Aunt Kelly, Aunt Natalie, and myself. Grandma looked good, glowing, having finally lost the weight she dreamed of losing in her lifetime.

Before we could watch the game, we had to wait in line to scan our tickets and get into Quicken Loans Arena, the "Q" as everyone in Cleveland likes to call it. Coincidentally, as we waited, a worship song began playing, and my eyes locked on her, waiting to see if and when she would put her hand up in praise.

Throughout waiting in line and watching the game from our suite, the colors of Wine and Gold surrounding us, the buzzer and various sound effects blaring in our ears, I couldn't get to her. I saw her smile down the row at me, a*nd words that have no form are falling from my lips.*

No words, no conversation. The impossibility that is present in both my dreams and in my reality. Even in my subconscious, I can't hear from her.

Lucinda

River flows.

East meets west, and together the eighty-five mile journey through urban and rural Ohio begins. It is distinguished by and named for its crooked nature, and on that winding path it finds its way.

And so Lucinda lives.

She is the firstborn of her parents, Bill and Polly. Followed by four more brothers and a stillborn baby girl, she is the first and only daughter. Southern blood in her veins, she grows up in the North, moving from city to suburb, from East to West. She finds God, thirsting for Him and taking whatever path she can, crooked or not, to seek and find Him, never able to get enough. She discovers the piano, she lives in books. She writes, the journals piling up.

She gets pregnant, gets married, and has her first baby, a son, at seventeen years old. The crooked path continues, through divorce and poverty, three more kids, a second marriage. Through weight gain, disease, hospitals, and IV drips, more medications to take. Adorned by red manicures, her brown hair died blonde, Juicy Fruit always in her purse, she becomes a grandmother, a widow. She lives alone and winds her way through life, her eyes fixed on Jesus, her faith sustaining her.

River flows, crooked as always, but still it flows and finds its way.

And so Lucinda lives.

II
Confluence

Rocking Chair

It sat under the archway, on the border between the den and the living room. If she was at my house and if she wasn't playing the piano or in the kitchen, I could find her sitting there. Rocking, surveying the activity of her family around her. Grabbing the remote and turning on Oprah or The View, whichever one was on.

And then she'd spot me. She'd tell me to grab a hair brush and stand in front of her. My brown hair was long and straight, falling all the way down my back for the entirety of my elementary school years. Grandma would brush it or run her manicured fingers through it. I remember both feeling relaxed by the sensation of her nails moving across my scalp and tickled by it, almost wanting to laugh. Once my hair was completely smooth and untangled, she'd braid it. Then I'd sit on her lap, rocking with her, leaning into her, watching a bunch of old ladies on the T.V. talk about stuff I didn't know anything about.

And sometimes I'd ask her to sing, and she would, always the same song:

I love you, a bushel and a peck, a bushel and a
peck,
aaaaaand
a hug around the neck, a hug around the neck
you betcha pretty heart I do,
do do do do do do, do do do do do do,
you betcha pretty heart I do.

And we'd keep rocking, her arm around my waist, my freshly-braided hair draped over my shoulder, the TV flashing as the commercials played. Rocking.

and lean not on your own understanding.

Dear Grandma,

As I'm growing up and learning how to be an adult, I find myself becoming more forgetful. Maybe it's because I have more to keep track of—rent, groceries, eighteen credit hours, two jobs, extracurricular commitments— I just find myself forgetting to text someone back, to buy toothpaste, to bring a book I promised to lend to someone.

I don't want to be forgetful, because sometimes it's more than just messages, more than something I wrote down in my planner that I hardly ever use.

I'm forgetting my experiences with you.

I can only remember a handful of things you ever said to me, and even those are a stretch since I'm unsure of their exact wording, besides a couple. When I was ten, I wasn't self-aware or aware of anything enough to realize the things I might want to remember just in case something were to happen. I lived completely in the moment, not thinking about death, never thinking that your obesity was destroying your body, wholeheartedly believing that everything was okay until Aunt Liz picked up the phone.

I'm forgetting the way your voice sounded. I can only recall your laugh. I don't remember how you interacted with your kids. I never looked for that kind of thing.

As I stood in the treehouse with Caity the day you died, as the mourners walked down the gravel driveway and drifted into the house, filling in the circle of crying and praying, I kept picturing you sitting on the bench at church. Blonde hair up in a clip, the flyaways wispy around your face. Black shirt, arms outstretched to me. Laughing, the white piece of gum looking like a tiny brain, resting visibly on your lower molars. I could smell the Juicy Fruit, see clearly the wrinkles around your brown eyes as you smiled. Amidst the people surrounding you, you were focused on me for that moment.

That's the image I conjured that day as my way to remember you and that's what I've held onto even since then. I never thought to remember you when you were alive. It was in the light of death that I realized the importance of holding onto things while my mind was still fresh with the memories.

The rest is just rememory, a word I learned from Toni Morrison's Beloved. *If you didn't read the book, I'm pretty sure you would have seen the movie because Oprah is in it. That whole book is strange and confusing, but I interpreted rememory as the memories we forgot that we had, that we remember for the second time. For all its weirdness, I still loved the book, by the way.*

My rememory hits me at random times. I forgot that you came to my dance recital until the song "These Dreams" by Heart came up on shuffle on my iPod. Sometimes walking barefoot in grass reminds me of your grave (I think Walt Whitman is partially to blame for that), and I remember leaving school on the first day of fifth grade to go to your funeral, Mrs. Becks comforting me. People met you, read about you, and they never forget you, even my teacher who never even knew you personally. The plastic dog from GiGi's house that now sits on my bookshelf reminds me that when I was little and both my parents were working, it was you who took care of me. I spent so much time with you but unfortunately, I was too little to remember it. I walk past the bench at church every week, but sometimes it's hearing the word "bishop" that reminds me of your Christian faith, the word you kept repeating as you were on your death bed. My dad says that it sounded more like "bis-sop" because your tongue was swollen from the fluid retention, but you kept saying it because you were so happy that Bishop Joey of The House of the Lord had come to visit you.

I don't trust my rememory completely though, because it's recalling the memories of a ten year old, already questionable in that regard, made all the more unreliable in the light of time that has passed. But it's nice when it comes.

I know that I remember your laugh correctly, though. I know that for sure every time I hear Aunt Natalie laugh.

Love,
Hanna Grace

Hi

I know

I'm a brown eyed girl and so are you

You're grounded

You need to say thank you

He wasn't trying to hurt your feelings he's just proud of
you

These are my favorite mattresses

Could you run the sweeper for me

Visit #3

It was a spring day in Cleveland, a time of the year when cold weather is still fair game. It was chilly, but the sun was shining so bright that we needed to wear sunglasses.

Senior year was drawing to a close, prom creeping up on the calendar. Unlike many other 17-year-old girls who had already done their shopping long ago, I still needed to find a dress, and unlike many other girls my age, I was avoiding following the current prom dress trends and instead searching for a vintage-style dress at a resale shop.

My Aunt Natalie, my Grandma, and I crossed the street to a row of shops. Grandma squealed like a little kid, so excited to be shopping for dresses.

I told my dad about the dream the next morning.

"She'd be going crazy if she were here right now," he said.

"Going crazy" is how my dad always describes how Grandma got excited about something. He said the same thing as he took pictures of me in my purple, mid-calf length, vintage dress as I got ready to go to prom for real. He said it again as we stood in my first apartment on Cleveland State's campus, a tiny studio that cost way too much. When the Cavs won the championship, *she'd be going crazy.*

If she were here.

She's missing my life. Our lives. But at least I know she'd be excited about it.

Hi

Every time I saw her. I don't remember it as *hello*, *hey*, *good morning*, nor anything else. Always *hi*, always drawn out to sound more like *hiiii*, always with a giant smile, always with arms outstretched. As she walked through the front door, as she sat at the bench at church, as we ran out to greet her at her car, *hiiii*.

Plastic Chair

"Grandma is as fat as a pig," I said to my dad. I was laying on our striped couch with him and laughing. I was probably around the age of four at the time, and somehow in my mind I thought my dad would think it was funny too.

I was wrong.

For the first time that I can remember, I saw my dad get mad. His eyebrows scrunched in fury like the diagonal lines I would draw on the eyebrows of stick figures to show that they were angry, he answered, "Don't you ever say that again!"

I stopped laughing.

My grandma was obese. I wasn't imagining or making it up. But after this conversation with my dad, I got used to her size. It was a part of who she was. I didn't think that it was anything worth talking or worrying about anymore.

One time I was jumping on the trampoline, I forget who with, and Grandma came out to watch. She grabbed a plastic chair that was aging and had started looking more brown than white as the paint chipped off and dirt accumulated. When she sat on it, it broke.

"Grandma!" I stopped jumping and rushed to the edge of the trampoline. "Are you okay?"

She nodded breathlessly as she moved amidst the broken plastic to stand up.

I don't know how she stood up, what she did with the pieces of the chair, or how she found another place to sit. I was no longer paying attention and had gone back to jumping.

It didn't occur to me that the fall had probably hurt her, that hitting the ground like that could have bruised her tailbone, or that the shards of broken plastic could have scraped her somewhere. I didn't think that her eyes could have been tearing up in embarrassment; after that conversation with my dad, I didn't think she had anything to be embarrassed about. Or maybe she was relieved that it was only two little kids who saw it happen. At that age, I hadn't learned yet that people tend to feel embarrassed when they fall, especially when they're overweight.

I Know

My sister, Amanda, was checked into the hospital the summer of 2006. Born prematurely with special needs, she's had unique and most of the time, unsolvable medical problems her whole life. This time she was catatonic. Not eating, not walking, not talking, and the doctors had no answers. We'd been spending almost every day of our summer break walking the pristinely clean, shiny hallways of the Cleveland Clinic until we found Amanda's room, our ears full of the sound of nurses' scrubs rustling together and the squeaky wheels of food carts carrying rubbery chicken, jello, and pills to patients. At eight and five years old, Jake and I didn't know how grave the situation was because adults don't disclose full details of a family crisis to children.

One day, things had taken a turn for the worst with Amanda, so the rest of our family came to visit and took up the entire waiting room, all aunts, uncles, cousins, and Grandma. My dad came to get me, and we walked to Amanda's room in the ICU. She had an oxygen mask on her face, ivy drips in her wrists, a white hospital gown on. Her eyes locked with mine when I walked in, and she started writhing, her back arching in her struggle as she made noises like she wanted to communicate something to me. I started crying, realizing that she couldn't even breath on her own and I could be losing her. When I got back to the waiting room, I went straight to Grandma. She held me in her arms, saying, "I know." Over and over again, "I know."

Gifts

Maybe I heard the sound of a car pulling up in the driveway or the sound of a door slamming; either way, something compelled me to run up to the living room window, and when I got there, I saw my Grandma walking up my driveway.

She was carrying a pink, plastic baton, the kind that has confetti swirling around on the inside, and a white McDonalds bag. I don't remember exactly what happened once that door was opened and she came inside, but I do know one thing for sure: Grandma gave me the baton, and it remains a fixture in my room to this day. Out of all the gifts I've gotten from her— the cards, the teddy bear, the books, the polka-dotted scarf— this baton remains the most visible, poking out from underneath my clothes every time I open my closet, reminding me of the day that Grandma came over bearing gifts.

On Christmas Eve of 2018, my family decided to watch old home videos. Actually, we didn't decide: it was my idea and everyone else went along with it. I wanted to see all of us when we were younger, our lives as they used to be, and I wanted to see Grandma.

The only device in our house that would hook up to our old camcorder was our dinosaur iMac monitor. So we placed it on a table in front of our couch, and we chose our first video: October 2003, Jake's second birthday.

My mom clicked the play button on the camcorder and the blue screen disappeared to reveal our house as it existed fifteen years ago. We saw the living room with its old white carpet, the walls covered in their former colors, toys scattered everywhere, not just because it was a birthday party, but because this was a house where two little kids lived. We also saw our family of fifteen years ago: some couldn't walk yet and instead crawled or were carried around by their parents; some had different hair colors (Aunt Natalie was blonde "for a minute" and apparently that minute was captured in this video); some hadn't arrived yet, and some were still alive.

My dad was behind the camera, and he was a fan of trying out the special effects on the camcorder. He used the fading-out effect as he moved from the kitchen, where most of the adults sat talking, to the living room where the kids were running around, crying, or checking out Jake's new toys. In present day 2018, my dad, sitting next to me on the couch, praises his camera work, calling himself a creative genius.

Back in the video, the camera moved away from the birthday boy banging on his new green, Leap Frog piano and singing (rather, making loud breathing noises) into the attached microphone and headed into the kitchen. My dad moved around the kitchen and got shots of everyone (even some of the little kids) saying "Happy Birthday Jacob" to the camera, except Grandma. She said, "Happy Birthday Jacob Thomas." The middle name that he shares with our dad and with Grandpa Kraker.

There are two things I'm reminded of in this seconds-long clip of Grandma: first, the sound of her voice. My memory hasn't remembered her voice exactly as it sounded. If I had my eyes closed while the video was playing, I would have known that it was her talking; but still, the exact tone of her voice is another thing that I've lost in my memories of her. That's what happens when you haven't heard something in a long time.

Second, I am reminded of how much she loved middle names. Most people are given middle names but they're hardly ever used unless you're from the South or you're in trouble and your parent calls you by your full name. Grandma used our middle names all the time. Maybe she wanted them to be put to good use, or maybe she just really loved them.

My parents named me Hanna without an *H* on

the end to be like my mom, Laura, and my sister, Amanda, whose names both end with an *A*. My dad also liked this spelling because of the Hanna Building and Hanna Theatre in downtown Cleveland. I know it's not the least common spelling of the name; but still, at gift shops I usually only find key chains or mini-license plates with *Hannah* on it, and none with the way my name is spelled.

My Grandma had the same problem: she wanted to get me a necklace that said my name, but they didn't have any with my spelling. She didn't give up, though: instead, she got me a necklace with *Grace* on it, my middle name, which she saw as a perfect solution. To her, Grace was as much a part of my name as Hanna.

Grandma loved our middle names, for all of their different meanings and significances, so I know that she didn't love the word *grace* just because it's my middle name. She loved this word because it goes went far beyond a name, far beyond a cluster of rainbow letters hanging from a chain. She knew that grace is something that reaches out to you in its perfect timing and takes root in your soul, and that from that moment on it guides your every step, transforming you as a person. And she lived this grace in all the ways that she was kind, encouraging, giving, faithful, and caring. She lived grace in her words, speaking to people in a way that showed that she valued them, even if that was simply calling her grandchildren by their first and middle names.

The best gifts are unexpected, and they are everywhere. Brennan Manning wrote that "grace proclaims the awesome truth that all is gift." When our lives our narrated by grace, we are are able to look around and see gifts where we hadn't seen them before. Oftentimes, these are the gifts that you don't unwrap; rather, you realize these gifts as they walk up your driveway and knock on the door, as you watch a home video and hear a voice you haven't heard in over ten years, or as a part of your identity from the very beginning awakens and whispers to your soul and calls you home.

I'm a brown eyed girl and so are you

Master Pizza, Center Road, Brunswick. Grandma's favorite restaurant. I was probably about seven years old. Our loud family took up booths and tables, the little kids not really paying attention to the tables that had been assigned to us or the other people in the restaurant. The jukebox was playing "Brown Eyed Girl" by Van Morrison, and Grandma was dancing in her seat, bopping along to the beat. She smiled, her eyes crinkling as she told me, "This song is about us, because I'm a brown eyed girl, and so are you."

Sha lalalalalalalalalala ti da.

These Dreams

I was nine years old and shy. So shy, that I didn't talk in dance class.

"Hanna, we're going to put you in this spot, okay?" Miss Jackie, my dance teacher pointed at the floor.

"That's fine," I whispered. I was so shy that when I had to speak during class, it was in a whisper.

We were beginning to learn our routine to the song "These Dreams" by Heart for our ballet number for the upcoming, eighties-themed recital in June. I didn't like the song, mainly because I had a typical nine-year old's taste in music centered around the top forty and the pop stars from Disney Channel, and thought the opening soundscapes of "These Dreams" were creepy and the singing sounded ugly.

We were being staged to make our entrance during these soundscapes and Miss Jackie had chosen me, as the shortest in the class, to lead the line out. Our costumes were long, flowy, white dresses with a purple sash around the middle, to embody the words of the song, *white skin in linen*. Sheer fabric from the dress attached to our wrists so that when we lifted our arms, we looked like we had angel's wings. In order to accentuate this feature of our costumes, we entered with our backs to the audience with our arms lifted high above our heads, taking small steps on pointe, circling around the stage to eventually face the front.

The dance came together over the next couple of months and suddenly, it was June.

Even on the night of dress rehearsal, after dancing with these girls for two hours a week over the entire past school year, I was still quiet. I felt insecure as the youngest girl on the team, intimidated by the confident girls who seemed so much older than me at thirteen and fourteen years old. I eventually befriended one girl on the team: Carly, the other shy girl.

While waiting for our turn to go on stage, I laid on the floor of the Brunswick High School classroom that we had transformed into our dressing room, reading a book while the rest of the girls goofed around, laughing at inside jokes that neither Carly nor I were apart of.

The time for our routine was coming, so we put on our costumes and ballet shoes and lined up. I was so shy, but strangely enough, I didn't feel nervous. I didn't feel any pressure to look perfect in front of the audience, even though my parents, my Aunt Natalie, and my Grandma were among them.

The song began, and I led the line of girls onstage. I went through the motions, although I didn't smile even though Ms. Jackie told me that I need to emote when I'm on stage.

The next morning, I poured Lucky Charms into a bowl and sat by my dad.

"Grandma cried watching you dance last night," he said.

"What?" I uncapped the milk jug and poured it into the cereal. "Why?"

"Because you led the line out onstage."

"Oh." I took my first bite.

"She said you looked like an angel," he said as I chewed on rainbow and shooting star-shaped marshmallows.

I could clearly picture her crying, just like my mom does in church: silently, lips pursed together to keep them from trembling, only giving away that they're crying when their hand repeatedly reaches up to wipe away the tears streaming down their cheeks. What I couldn't understand was how she found some sort of tear-jerking beauty in something I was so shy about, something I saw no significance in.

That same day, my Aunt Natalie pulled into our driveway and I ran through the front yard barefoot to greet her, my feet unbothered by the gnarled roots of the trees that spread throughout the grass. To my surprise, my Grandma got out of the passenger side.

I don't remember exactly what she said, curse my faulty rememory. But she said it all when she handed me a gift bag on a day that wasn't Christmas or my birthday.

"Oh my God, Hanna, you were the best one up there," Aunt Natalie said as she comes around the car to join us. "You led the rest of the girls out onstage."

"No, I wasn't," I replied quickly, though I still smiled because Aunt Natalie's gushing always made me feel special. I opened the bag and pulled out a teddy bear dressed in a pink tutu and pair of ballet shoes, and a picture frame that had a pair of ballet shoes in the corner and curtains draped around the glass, designed to make who ever was in the picture frame look like they were onstage.

"Thank you," I said to Grandma as she wrapped me in a hug, her usual greeting.

The teddy bear sat on my bed for a long time, and now it resides in the bottom drawer of my dresser. The picture frame contains one of the two pictures I have of just me with Grandma: I'm about two years old sitting at the table at GiGi's (our nickname for Grandma's mom, short for "great grandmother") house, a half-eaten cookie sits in my hand. Grandma leans behind me in a purple shirt, a soft grin on her face. She didn't smile with her teeth very often.

The footage for the Recital DVD was taken the night of dress rehearsal. I can put the DVD in, fast forward to my ballet routine, and be a member of the audience with her. I cry along with her, knowing that she's crying too, watching nine-year old me lead the line of girls out onto the stage, though we cry for different reasons.

You're grounded

I sat on my Uncle Chris's couch as he talked on the phone. He was watching Jake and me because Amanda was in the hospital, that same summer of 2006. He hung up the phone with one word, "Fuck." I gasped, and he tried to convince me that he had really said, "Fluck." But I knew what I heard, and the next time I saw Grandma, I told on him. "You're grounded," she told him jokingly, and I wished she was being serious.

Dear Grandma,

I remember you laying in your mother's bed. GiGi was dying, and you and Aunt Natalie were laying on either side of her, crying as you both cleaned her teeth.

I remember going out to dinner. My family and you went to The Streetside Cafe on Pearl Road in Medina, which has been closed for years now. On the spring night we went the weather was beautiful, so we sat outside on the deck. A lady came up to our table, and I figured it was one of your old friends. When she walked away, my dad told me that she was Paul Jackson's second ex-wife. So, not an old friend. Other people would have made that situation awkward, would have avoided eye contact, but you were nice to everyone. You didn't hold grudges, you weren't prejudiced. You loved like Jesus does.

I remember sitting at a family party in our basement and telling you a joke, and nothing about it was funny. I don't remember the joke exactly, but I remember saying something about the word "ain't" not being in the dictionary, and at one point I quoted Hannah Montana's dad from the Disney Channel show, and said, "woo doggy", his catchphrase. Like I said: not funny at all. But you laughed anyways.

I remember the books. Stacks of journals, Bibles with your highlighting in them, romantic novels scattered throughout your house. One night at church during band rehearsal, I came up to where you were sitting at the piano and I told you that I wanted historical fiction books for my birthday which was coming up. You got me two books about a girl named Maddie living during the American Revolution. I started them but never finished, which I feel bad about, because you came through and I didn't. But at least they're still sitting on my bookshelf. One day when I was about to start my first year of college at Cleveland State, I was sitting with my dad in his truck, and he told me that he believes that if you had gone to college, you would've been an English major, too. You loved books and you loved writing. Sometimes I wonder what you'd think about me writing about you. When I doubt that you would like it, I remember that you did the same thing by keeping journals for us. I also wonder if you would have came to all those midnight premieres for the Twilight movies with the rest of us, but that's a different topic.

I remember going to the House of the Lord with you, Emily, Caity, and Amanda. It was summertime, and there was a block party after service, tables set up everywhere with games to play, hot dogs on the grill. One man was handing out bracelets that had the letters "WWJD?" on them. I asked you what they meant, and you told me that they stood for "What Would Jesus Do?" with a smile. I put the bracelet on.

I remember the day Zoey was born. We were all gathered in the hospital room and I was holding her. After a couple minutes, you took her. I wanted to keep holding her but there was no way I was going to say no to you.

I remember one morning after a sleepover at your house, waiting for our parents to come pick us up. I took a book out of my bag that I had brought with me: God's Wisdom for Little Girls: Virtues and Fun from Proverbs 31. *I showed you the book and read the title to you, but I said Proverbs wrong, pronouncing it like the pro in pro sports. You taught me the right way to say it.*

I remember you laying in your bed. That summer morning while Amanda was in the hospital and you were watching us, Jake and I were trying to sleep in the living room but failing, afraid of the ghosts that we feared were lurking around us. I tiptoed down the hall to see if you were awake yet, but I just saw you laying there and didn't want to disturb you, sleeping or not.

I remember, and that's how I continue to find you, how I remind myself that I knew you, that I still know you now. Loss, though it hurts, is constructive in that it teaches us the value of remembering, because in holding onto our memories, even the seemingly ordinary or unimportant ones, we are able to hold onto those we've lost and we are able to feel close to them again. I can't come over your house, sit on the couch and talk to you, or call you on the phone. What I can do is write, think, and imagine. Though these options aren't as ideal as having you physically here with us, it does make me feel closer to you in a new way that I didn't feel when I was ten.

These moments with you that I do remember, Grandma, are so uneventful. They are the simplest of encounters, tiny snippets of the time I knew you. But I treasure them all the same, because they bring me back to you.

I remember, and I pray to never forget.

Love,
Hanna Grace

Visit #2

Jake and I were orphans. Grandma was the one who saved us.

She came silently, looking exactly as she did in her prom photo: brown hair, up in a beehive, the only difference in that she came alone and in casual clothes. Young. Not the Grandma we knew. She took us to Pennsylvania, as Ohio apparently wasn't the place for us to live anymore.

We shopped at Home Depot for wood to build our new house for our new life. Jake and I wandered around, his young, skinny self dressed in a plaid shirt, bony elbows jutting out as he grabbed onto the cart, pushed off the floor and rode down the aisle.

She didn't say a word. She just stood there, watching us.

Despite the tragedy that we had obviously faced that resulted in Jake and I becoming orphans and losing the other three members of our family unit, it wasn't a nightmare.

You need to say thank you

My ninth birthday. My entire family watching as I opened my presents in our kitchen, I was told to close my eyes and I obliged, covering them with my hands for good measure. When I given the okay to open them, I looked to see my dad holding a brand new purple bike in his hands.

"Wow!" I said, trying to be funny. "How much was it?"

Once the party was winding down, I was walking by my grandma when she reached out and grabbed my arm, pulling me towards her. "Your mom and dad got you a nice gift. You need to say thank you." That was the only lecture that I can remember getting from her.

Dear Grandma,

I visited your grave yesterday. I would say I visited you, but a headstone bearing your name and marking where your body lies six feet underneath the ground is not you. As C.S. Lewis said, "You do not have a soul. You are a soul. You have a body." I visited your body, but not you.

Just as I felt when I revisited your house, I pulled up into Eastlawn Memorial Gardens on Grafton Road and everything seemed so much smaller than when I was younger. Maybe it was the effect of the leafless trees or the addition of new subdivisions to the outskirts of the cemetery; either way, the lawns dotted with headstones and flower wreaths that once seemed endless now seemed flat and contained— some trees, rocks, and statues stuck in the middle of the suburban sprawl.

I stopped on my way to church, because I'm still working there. It's been better lately, but I still don't plan on going into ministry as my career even though my dad is convinced otherwise. I guess things could always change, but that's where I'm at right now.

It's Easter weekend so I was dressed up, wearing heels, my hair curled, the smell of hairspray reaching my nostrils whenever the wind blew.

Parking my car, I got out and found your grave towards the back of the veterans' section because you share a plot with Grandpa Kraker. The ground still soft and muddy as Ohio is making a very long transition from winter to spring, my heels sunk into the ground with every step. But I wasn't annoyed. I was too distracted by scanning every headstone I passed, looking for your name because it's been a while and I couldn't remember exactly where you and Grandpa lie. I finally found your grave, the flat, marble stone flush with the ground, and while I wanted it to be a profound, sweet moment, my words upon visiting your body for the first time in years and by myself were neither profound nor sweet; rather, they were: "That sucks. What the hell?"

    Grandpa's side, which reads "Big Al" across the top with the years 1942-1998 in the middle, the emblem of a motorcycle at the bottom, was fine, clean. But your side seemed to have sunken in the ground a bit, the first letters of your name, "Luc", all that was visible until the rest of the stone disappears into a puddle of water, brown maple leaves floating around in the murk.

    Before taking action, I stood in front of the stone, scrolling through iTunes on my phone. I put on an Elvis song, "Return to Sender" for you, and then I went to the edge of the woods and broke a stick off of a tree branch. I walked back, shoes accumulating more mud, and used the stick to drag the leaves off. Within seconds I could finally see the rest of the stone.

I couldn't do anything about the water, so I looked through it to read "Sandie" across the top, "Lucinda Faye Kraker 1948-2008" across the center, a golden piano at the bottom. I forgot about that piano. It really is a nice touch.

I'm sorry I didn't bring anything to lay on it, that I all I could do was take the withered, cracked leaves off. No flowers, no cross, no American flag. I was thinking about bringing chocolate, but all we had were chocolate chips at home and that just didn't seem classy to me. Little squirrels and rabbits or nasty raccoons would be coming to eat off your grave.

After Elvis was over, I put on "Hallelujah What a Savior" by Tommy Walker. Our church band does it every year on Easter, and every year I look forward to it. My dad, Uncle Bill, and the singer Michele performing it is the best song our church does, in my opinion. It's especially powerful on Easter, because the sanctuary is packed, as more people come to church on Easter than any other Sunday of the year. They usually play it after the sermon, so everyone is still in their seats. As the song progresses, people start to stand up in the crowd, until the entire room is standing, some people putting their hands up, myself included. I used to be too self-conscious to do that, but now I don't care. My dad always says that when it comes to worship, the only person you need to worry about is yourself. Then when they get to the bridge, "oh when He comes, our glorious King", the people back in the tech booth raise the shades on the windows, so the room is filled with light. I know it's coming, but still, I get chills every time.

I can't say if they ever played it while you were still alive because I don't know; nonetheless, I know that you would have loved it, too. So that's why I played it for you, and that's why I cried a little bit as the words, "Full atonement, can it be? Hallelujah what a savior" emitted from my low-quality iPhone speaker. Because I wish you were here to hear it, that you were among the people standing in the crowd raising your arms as the light enters the room and all of our voices join together.

I love that song, because as I tell everyone after the song is finished each Easter service, that is what I think Heaven will be like. Voices singing, hands raised, the light shining. Glory.

The song ended, I kissed my fingers, touched your grave, and then turned around and left.

Happy Easter. This weekend we celebrate what you get to celebrate every day, if there are even days any more where you are.

Love,
Hanna Grace

He wasn't trying to hurt your feelings, he's just proud of you

Church, a rare Sunday where Doc was out and my dad was the one preaching. I was sitting with Aunt Natalie, Amanda, and Grandma, who had made us sit in the front row, right in front of my dad. I couldn't pay attention because sermons were boring to me, but my ears perked up at the mentioning of my name, and I tuned right in as my dad said, "My daughter Hanna is growing up, but she's still my little princess. Every time I see her walking around the house, she's just like a princess." I was mortified, thinking to myself, *he's telling the whole church that I play dress up! I don't do that anymore. Everyone is going to think I'm a stupid girly-girl.*

After the service ended, I ran to the preschool classrooms and started crying, an inconsolable nine-year old girl surrounded by a bunch of happy two-year olds playing with toys, eating Goldfish, and learning that Jesus loves them. Everyone tried to calm me down, but no one succeeded. Not even Grandma could get me to stop crying as she told me, "He wasn't trying to hurt your feelings, he's just proud of you."

She didn't seem very sympathetic either, as she was more focused on how proud she was of her son and his preaching.

A little while later, I realized that my dad said that because the night before that Sunday, I had sat next to him as he wrote his sermon, reading *The Little Princess* by Frances Hodgson Burnett. It was a misunderstanding. I haven't heard him mention me in a sermon since.

Dear Grandma,

I forget what I wanted to write.

Normally when I think of something, I create a note of it in my phone or write it down somewhere, because I know I'll forget it. But maybe something about this idea seemed unforgettable, because as I bounced along in the back row of the golf cart my dad was driving down a gravel road on Kelley's Island, the dust kicked up into a cloud around us as we accelerated, I didn't feel the need to write it down. As the dust stung my eyes, the dirt covered my feet and settled in a gray layer on my knock-off, Target-bought Birkenstocks, I couldn't wait to write because I knew it would be good.

I remember the details, but I don't remember my bottom line, what connected all these thoughts and images together.

The first of my thoughts was the significance of being back on Kelley's Island. As we pulled into the ferry dock, we saw people all wearing matching t-shirts, getting ready to spend a week at Camp Patmos just as I did so many years ago.

The second was that this is the place where Joe and Caity got engaged. As we drove through tiny downtown areas, past historic buildings and vacation homes, I would see an expanse of beach and wonder, is that where it happened?

The third was the excitement of learning

something new about you. We stopped at an art gallery, the yard full of abstract metal sculptures, where we met a woman named Cynthia, the wife of the artist. Somehow my dad got to talking about you with her, saying how your name was Lucinda and your nickname was Cindy, but because your relatives in Alabama had such a thick southern accent, whenever they called your name it sounded like Sandie, not Cindy. So now that mystery is solved for me.

Now, I'm disappointed because I thought writing this out would help me remember that bottom line, help me figure out what I was getting at, that revelation I had on the golf cart.

We go through life experiencing new things every day, always remembering and forgetting. There's no way to hold onto it all. I could do with forgetting the names of some of the celebrities and reality stars I hear about, forgetting the way my clothes looked that one day, forgetting that he said that, that stupid thing I did— but you can't choose what you forget. Usually it's the things you want to cling to that slip away, the things that you try to forget that linger. Of all the ten years I had with you, I've remembered special moments which I'm thankful for, but I've also remembered extremely strange things: for example, I remember that one time I walked into the church bathroom and you were peeing in the first stall. Every time I look at the first stall, I think of you. How weird is that? I'd rather know what we talked about when you came over with the baton and McDonalds bag in your hand, but I can't exchange that memory for another one. You peeing in the first stall is one of my memories of you that I'm left with.

I just prayed to God to help me remember. I've started praying to Him about everything throughout the day, trying to pray without ceasing as the Apostle Paul instructs us to do. Last night, it was me praying at three a.m. for Him to help me find motivation to finish my capstone paper for my French major that was due today. Sometimes it's praying for breakthrough in someone's life, for racism to end, for peace to prevail; other times, it's the trivial things that won't change anyone's world but my own.

Remembering and forgetting. I can't remember what filled my brain, what energized me earlier and made me wish I had my laptop with me.

A few days later, I finally remembered: I wanted to know your testimony beyond what you wrote in Cindy Lu, your story of faith; at least, how you would tell it, because the key moment in my testimony happened on Kelley's Island.

One day towards the end of the spring semester, I was at Edgewater Park with my friend, Ruth, who is from the Democratic Republic of the

Congo. We were walking along the path that bisects the giant hill that leads to the beach, the Cleveland Skyline behind us and the lake stretching out next to us. She was telling me a little bit about her time spent in refugee camps before she came to America.

After listening to her stories, I blurted out, "I wish I had an awesome testimony story."

"What are you talking about?" Ruth asked. "Jesus saved you!"

How right she was. No matter how our individual testimonies differ, we all testify to the same, awesome truth: Jesus saves. It's not about us or what we've done. It's all and only about Him.

God wrote my story, weaving together all of the events that brought me to Him. Why should I ask Him to change it?

My testimony begins with being a music pastor's daughter, watching a church grow and expand, dancing along to worship songs, playing air guitar as I sing the words, "I am free" along with Caity during our Sunday morning kids' service. And being on Kelley's Island again, I can't help but think back to those years of camp. Just as John met God on the island of Patmos, so I met Him at my own Patmos. That chapel is where I sensed the Holy Spirit for the first time, that corner of the beach over there is where I accepted Christ into my life, the savior who kneels to wash the dirt off of our feet.

My faith journey is the high school years, reading His word and falling in love. It's working in ministry, frustrated with my situation, wishing it was easier. It's writing this, trying to be vulnerable, telling your story, wondering what God could do with this.

I know the events of your life, but they've been told to me through others. The story you wrote about your childhood, "Cindy Lu", gave me insight into how you began your faith journey, but that's only a small piece of your testimony. I want to know how you relied on God throughout being a teenage mom, a divorcee at twenty-two, through poverty, through failing health. I want to know the verses that helped you, how you started going to the House of the Lord in Akron, how through everything that happened to you, you found joy and you kept putting your hand up.

But I do know the only part that really matters of any testimony: Jesus saved you. You went through a lot while I feel like I've gone through next to nothing. But through everyone's story, no matter how they differ in their events, we are united by the cross, knowing that He loves us and has woven us a story, and we get to walk in His grace and mercy through it all.

Love,

Hanna Grace

p.s.

Guess what Caity told me at Uncle Bill's birthday party tonight? She and Joe got engaged on Put-in Bay, not Kelley's Island.

These are my favorite mattresses

A girls getaway, Grandma was taking four of her granddaughters to a hotel for a sleepover and church at the House of the Lord the next day. We checked into our room at the Hampton Inn, went swimming, and then got ready for bed.

As we turned out the lights and divided ourselves up between the two queen beds, Grandma said "These are my favorite mattresses." I felt special because I was the one sleeping next to her.

Patio Couch

My Uncle Bill's birthday falls on August fifteenth, and as the date of the first day of school continued to creep up earlier in August each year, his party came to signify the end of summer. This birthday had a greater cause for celebration than others because it was his fortieth, a new decade.

In the middle of the increasingly suburban Strongsville, Ohio, my Uncle Bill, my Grandma's second child, and Aunt Liz had a huge backyard. In the back by the woods was a tree house that was worthy of royalty, a grape vine, and a hammock to lay and swing in. Towards the house was the patio, where concrete paths weaved through flower patches and bushes, towards the doors to the house and the grill, where smoke rose to the sky as Aunt Liz opened the cover to reveal the hamburgers and hot dogs we would later be feasting on.

Grandma settled herself on a wooden patio couch covered with red cushions. I can't remember what she was wearing, but I remember her blonde hair hanging loose around her shoulders.

The next time I'd see her, she'd be lying in a casket.

Every time I went to Uncle Bill and Aunt Liz's house thereafter, I'd look at that patio couch through the window or walk by it when I was outside. I'd see the wrinkles and the way it sagged in the middle, and think that it was that way because she had sat there. The seat seemed to be permanently holding its breath with no hope of exhale. To me, it was an artifact, an imprint left by her to remind me of the last time I saw her alive.

When Words Fail

Music speaks.

In Grandma's steadily emptying house, the living room rid of everything besides a lamp without a lampshade and her electric piano, Uncle Chris taught me "Alone" by Heart on the piano. I've been taught a lot of songs on the piano over the years and forgotten most of them, but never this one.

Grandma was the piano player in the family. Of my generation, Caity was the one to take after her. I remember Grandma sitting in the front row at her piano recital, crying as Caity played a couple songs. One year, Grandma even gave her piano to her, and I don't know if there could have been a more special gift for her to give to anyone.

I was inspired at one point in my life to learn the piano for real, and I asked Grandma to teach me. The next time she came over my house, she brought a packet over titled "Hanna Grace's Piano Lessons" with a ballerina stamped in the corner since I was a dancer. For our first lesson, she found a blank page in the packet and traced my hands in purple crayon, so I could remember how to place them on the piano and the names of the notes that each finger should rest on. Then she taught me how to do to finger runs, placing my thumb on Middle C, the rest of my fingers on the proceeding keys. I remember her pointing out that middle C was the most important key on the piano, which would be easy for me to remember because the C in Cambridge, the brand name of our piano, was printed right above it. She taught me a song to sing with this scale, and we sang along together as she helped me: *little river flowing, flowing, little river flowing, downward toward the sea.* That was the only lesson we ever had, but I still remember what she taught me all these years later, so she obviously was a good teacher.

I've never been committed to any of my musical endeavors over the years: piano lessons were short-lived, I played flute in the middle school band but stopped when I started high school, my parents got me a ukulele for Christmas one year but I never learned to play it, and all the bands I started with Caity never lasted long. That last one is a shame, though, because I honestly believe that our band, "Nostalgic Inferno", could have really made it big, solely because of the badass name. The only artistic sphere that I've always been committed to is reading and writing.

This led to me having an argument with my

dad about if music or writing is the highest form of art. It wasn't going well for me.

Running out of ammunition, I asked, "Which class is required throughout your entire education: English or music?"

My dad looked at me, a smile spreading across his face, and said, "When words fail, music speaks," and pointed both his fingers at me in the shape of guns, as if to say *boom, I won.* Which he did. I couldn't think of any comeback to that.

There's a picture of him and Grandma on her old couch, the one she must have had before the leather couches that I remember. Next to Grandma was a pillow that had these very words embroidered on it.

It turns out that it was a writer who originally said that: Hans Christian Andersen, who penned fairy tales and fables, such as *The Little Mermaid* and *The Ugly Duckling.* Even a writer had to admit that music has the power to communicate when words cannot. Though I don't like to lose arguments, I have to admit that it's true: music speaks.

Sitting next to me in the nosebleeds, my mom cries as Paul McCartney and the entirety of Quicken Loans Arena sing "Hey Jude" together. I sang the "Na Na"s along with the crowd at the top of my lungs, waving my phone above my head with the flashlight on, relishing in the fact that I was in the same room as a Beatle.

When she was in the hospital and catatonic, the song "Bubbly" by Colbie Callait made Amanda smile.

At family parties and gatherings, at any point, one of the kids would ask Grandma to play the piano, usually the Boogie Woogie. It was always possible for her to do this since every household in our family had a piano. She'd oblige every time, happy to play for us. I don't think there's ever been a time when my dad has heard her play it, or tried to play it himself, and not mentioned how he cannot believe her fingers were able to work like that across the keys, her hands playing two such opposite things at the same time.

Every year, our church's band puts on a Christmas show that has turned into quite a production throughout the fifteen years of its existence. Grandma played piano in the show while she was alive, and the year she died, the show was dedicated to her. My dad always tries to change up the songs, and in recent years, he's added "Christmas Tears" by Freddie King, as a tribute to Grandma. Before they start the song, an old polaroid photo appears on the screen. Uncle Bill and my dad stand on opposite sides of Grandma, kissing her on the cheek as she smiles at the camera. Underneath the photo, she wrote "My Boys" in her trademark cursive. Either my dad or Uncle Bill introduce her and tell the audience that they're dedicating the song to her.

"The holidays are tough when you've lost someone," Uncle Bill says after the picture shows on the screen. It must have been his turn this year. "We lost our mom, and this time of year... well, we miss her." He keeps his composure, but you can tell it's hard for him to talk about.

The song begins, and that's when their emotions are unleashed. When all the words they couldn't say, couldn't find, are expressed. Uncle Bill plays bass and belts out the song, my dad has a guitar solo. The song builds, my dad keeps shredding, Uncle Bill is bopping along, completely absorbed in the music. On the inside they're crying Christmas tears, and words fail in that moment. Music is what speaks for them.

It's moments like these that make me realize that my dad was right: music creates moments, unites people, and communicates in ways that words cannot, because sometimes there are no words. It can be difficult to express all that life encompasses. If you really want to understand my family, to see all the joy, unity, love, and for the past ten years, the grief, look to the music. It will tell you all about it.

Peach Picking

I climbed into my Aunt Liz's van. It had blue and white stripes around the outside and felt like a living room on the inside even though it wasn't an RV. The middle row was comprised of two blue, plush seats that were like armchairs. They swiveled and everything. The back seat was like a couch, but I stayed away from it because it was the domain of my cousin Joe, Emily and Caity's younger brother, and it wasn't uncommon to find a chicken nugget or plastic toys stuck between the cushions. There was a TV in between the driver's and passenger's seat that we watched to make the long car ride go faster. *Little Shop of Horrors* seemed to be the only movie they kept in there.

Aunt Liz took us to a peach tree farm in what felt like the middle of nowhere. I didn't realize it at the time, but this was probably her way of distracting us since Grandma had been in the hospital since Uncle Bill's birthday party and we kept asking about when we could see her. My mom was doing the same thing with Jake and Joe by taking them swimming for the day.

We climbed out of the air conditioned van and walked through the parking lot. The August sun beat down on us and caused us to squint, our eyebrows attempting to be enough shade for our eyes. We grabbed our baskets and meandered down the seemingly endless rows of trees underneath the cloudless sky, choosing our peaches with care. The branches were low so I could easily pick out the peaches I wanted, the least fuzzy and the least bruised ones. We picked those reddish orange fruits with hopes of eating them later, peeling them and dicing them, maybe even making a pie.

August 20, 2008. Summer was almost over. We kept picking peaches.

Could you run the sweeper for me?

Different summer, same situation: Amanda was in the hospital. Not nearly as bad as two summers ago, she'd be back home within a couple weeks. In the meantime, instead of taking us to the hospital with her, one morning my mom decided to deposit Jake and me at Grandma's house at six a.m. She answered the door, and after we were settled on the couch with blankets, she went back to her room to sleep. I took the bigger couch since I was the older sister, but I couldn't fall back asleep. I was too afraid of the ghosts that lived there according to my dad and uncles, so I laid on my back and stared at the ceiling, telling myself over and over again that ghosts don't exist, that at ten years old I shouldn't be such a scaredy cat anymore.

Once Grandma was awake again, we got a glimpse into her daily life as we endured watching Oprah and The View, sitting on the couches in our pajamas the entire morning. We were bored but we didn't complain.

She eventually got up and went to the kitchen, and called the two of us in there. "Could you run the sweeper for me?" she asked, breathless, handing me the cord. I may not be able to remember a lot of the words she ever said to me, but I can clearly remember that sound of her being out of breath, a sound that often accompanied her words.

A couple months later, we'd be sitting on those same couches, but in a house she no longer lives in. After a day of the entire family working together to pack up the house, my family unit plus Aunt Natalie remained. The living room lit by the harsh light of lamps without shades, we sat in a circle as my dad read aloud one of her journals.

After that morning we spent at her house, she wrote, "Today, Hanna and Jacob came over. They watched TV with me and even helped me clean the kitchen. They are such angels!"

A tear slid down my cheek as I stared across the room at the line where the wall meets the floor and thought to myself, *we didn't do anything special but she still thought we were angels. She's the one who's really an angel anyways.*

Hanna

River burns.

For all the years and events that came before, this erases all and becomes the legacy. Polluted, black and slick with oil, yellow toxic signs posted, smoke rises from the water.

And so Hanna remembers.

The things that matter most burn, the kind of fire that she stokes, fears when it will be snuffed out. These strongest fires are the gifts, the music, the laugh, the Juicy Fruit, the hugs, the piano, the handwriting. Some fires have been put out long ago. Like smoke, so many words have risen and drifted away. But sometimes they come back, in a scorch mark, the flick of a match being lit, in ashes, and the fire burns again. Burning to hold on, to never lose this flame again, to remember, craving to know more.

The legacy she remembers is faith, the strongest fire of them all. The fire that burned for God, the only fire she would want to be remembered for. The soul that burned to know Him, to serve Him, to love Him with all her mind, heart, soul, and strength.

Sometimes burning feels more like yearning, sometimes fire gives life rather than destroys it.

River burns, its legacy staying put while the smoke rises.

And so Hanna remembers.

III
Mouth

Like a River Flows

I'm not the one who heard her say it. Caity told me.

I recalled those words as I was getting my hair done and an Elvis song began, filling the entire room from the mini Bluetooth speaker on the coffee table, surrounded by assortments of Oreos, fruits, hairspray, and bobby pins.

We were all sitting there in our church's meeting room, which doubles as the bridal suite on wedding days. Dispersed throughout the room, dressed in flannels and sweatpants or shorts, Aunt Natalie was putting makeup on Aunt Liz, my friend Kayla was doing my hair. Other bridesmaids did their own makeup or were already ready, aside from getting dressed. Our dresses hung from the top of the white board that Doc used to direct staff meetings and theology classes during the week. We were all pretty quiet, keeping to ourselves.

I can't wait.

The day that we've all been excited for arrived way quicker than expected, but isn't that how time always works? It moves slow and fast, both trudging in its footsteps and flying at the same time. When she told me what Grandma said, this day seemed impossibly far in the future. We didn't even know who the groom would be. Even when Joe and Caity got engaged, nearly a year and a half before their wedding day, this day seemed so far. But 2017 turned to 2018, the months and days going by until October 6 arrived. Every Saturday for the past couple months, I've sent a text to Caity, counting down the weeks until the wedding. Waking up the morning of their wedding day, driving to church, the rain falling outside taken as a sign that Joe and Caity will one day be rich, the event seemed still seemed far away. It seemed impossible that it could already be here, that we could already be at the phase of our lives when the people we grew up with are getting married.

To see you girls.

We were all together in that room. Not all at the same time, but all of the women in the family passed through at some point during Caity's final moments as a Kraker. I was in my own corner of the room as Kayla jammed another bobby pin onto my head when Zoey came and sat down on the couch next to me. She handed me Oreos when I asked for some since I couldn't move to reach them while being restrained by the curling iron, but besides that, we really didn't talk. But when that Elvis song came on, we both sang along together, *Like a river flows, surely to the sea, darling so it goes, some thing are meant to be.* Zoey handed me a golden Oreo as Kayla baptized my curls in several blasts of hairspray. We kept singing, *Take my hand, take my whole life too, for I can't help falling in love with you.* The younger cousins who weren't in the wedding party still wore burgundy, the color of the bridesmaid dresses. They took selfies with each other and posted them on Instagram.

Walk down the aisle.

It's fitting that Caity was the one Grandma said these words to, being that she was the first one to get married. This was the first trip down the aisle that Grandma missed.

And although Grandma was not sitting in the audience, wiping away tears, wearing purple as Aunt Liz said she would have if she were there, she didn't miss it. Like a river flows, we move forward from source to mouth, carrying all that's come before along with us. Like a river flows, we have many branches, coming together at a confluence in some moments, separating at others, joining back together eventually or never again. Sometimes the river is deep, other times it's shallow and clear. There are periods of rapids, times of stillness. Sometimes there are sharp bends; sometimes the path is simple and unhurried; and sometimes, there are falls that no matter how hard you fight against them, they will pull you over. This life is full of the unexpected but one thing is for certain: like a river flows, we are all going towards what is meant to be, and what has always been. Surely, we are. The river we are all going down is a temporary journey on its way to the eternal. At every moment, the people we've lost and our memories of the past are with us. They might have reached the sea before us, but their role is never finished.

So, no, Grandma was not alive and breathing on October 6, 2018, the first wedding of one of her granddaughters. She did not see Caity walk down the aisle, nor will she ever see any of us girls take that walk that we are all looking forward to. But we cannot believe for a moment that she wasn't there, because she was.

She was there, as Caity said her vows, as she held Joe's hands and became his wife. In the gold anklet Caity wore, the gold bracelet I wore as I watched from my place in the bridesmaid's line on stage, both pieces of Grandma's jewelry that we took from her house after she died. She was present in the piece of paper that fell from Caity's aunt's Bible, which turned out to be a note that Grandma had written years before, some words from the book of Isaiah copied down in her loopy cursive. When Elvis played on the speaker, when my dad and I shared a chocolate bar as we headed towards the reception, when all of her kids, grandkids, and youngest brother Donny danced to the Isley brothers, lifting up our arms every time we heard the word "Shout!", dancing and singing along together.

Rivers travel for many miles, through many landscapes. Throughout the entire journey and all of its changes, there are two points that remain the same: the source and the mouth. We have no control over what happens in the middle, no idea when to expect stillness, rapids, or when confluences are going to come together or separate; but, from her vantage point in the sea, Grandma is watching us. She sees us. And surely, one day, we will make it there too.

In all your ways acknowledge him,

Dear Grandma,

You never got to see me love Jesus. You didn't see a lot of things that happened and you won't get to see the milestones later on in my life but my faith is the thing I care most about, because it's what you lived your life for.

I moved to Lakewood about five months ago. I wanted to commute from home this year but my dad said that I needed to learn to be an adult, so he found me an apartment in Lakewood, the top floor of his friend's duplex on Cove Avenue. Then August came around and the apartment fell through, too close to the school year for comfort. As the first day of school loomed closer on the calendar, I feared that I would never find an apartment and that I would let down the girl who was going to be my roommate.

You never got to see me love Jesus. You weren't in the audience when I stepped into the tub on the church stage with Caity when I was thirteen years old. Surprised at how warm the water was, I moved to stand next to my dad as he put one hand on my shoulder and his other on Caity's. He asked us the customary questions and dunked us, buried in the likeness of Christ's death. You didn't cheer with the crowd as we came back up again, raised in the power of His resurrection. You didn't get a piece of cake at our baptism party afterwards at Uncle Bill and Aunt Liz's house.

We found an apartment, the top floor of a duplex on Granger Avenue, the street name a good omen because I'm a huge Harry Potter fan (I've come a long way since I watched The Sorcerer's Stone *at your house when I was six years old and was subsequently terrified of all things Harry Potter for my remaining elementary and middle school years), and moved in the day before school started. My favorite part of the entire place is that it's old. I just think that old buildings have so much more character than new, trendy homes with their granite countertops and plush carpet. Right now I'm sitting on my couch and staring out the front window that's painted white with wooden, square panes across the glass, a Christmas wreath hanging over it even though it's the end of January. A pink glow over the rows of houses and the silhouettes of bare tree branches shows evidence of a sunset that fights to reveal itself against the snowstorm that's brewing.*

You didn't get to see me love Jesus. Really love Him. I was a freshman in high school when I fell in love with the book of Romans and began a pursuit of God daily. I woke up each day excited for those moments I'd spend reading the Bible, His word my bread of life. I never got to talk to you about the ideas I was amazed by or show you the verses I'd underlined or explain to you the peace and joy I was feeling that passed all understanding, although I'm

156

sure you would have understood perfectly.

The porch swing slams against the wall outside as the wind blows. I can't tell if it's snowing anymore or if the wind is just blowing the already-fallen snow around. I pull my blanket tighter around me, the apartment set at fifty-nine degrees, as we're college students who'd rather be a little cold than pay a higher gas bill.

You never got to see me love Jesus because you're not here. That's what breaks my heart the most when I think of the way we could have been. Because faith was what you lived for, and now it's what I live for.

Love,

Hanna Grace

Polly Pockets

After getting back from peach picking, Emily, Caity, and I resumed our never-ending game of Polly Pockets, pulling the rubber clothes onto their tiny, plastic bodies, using Joe's action figures, such as Luke Skywalker and Ben 10 (at church we used the Jesus figurine), as our dolls' boyfriends. We needed a break from the boredom of the car ride, and the exhaustion of picking the peaches in the sun, so we played dolls for a little while before beginning the next phase of our peach extravaganza, whatever it was that Aunt Liz had planned for us to do with them.

In the midst of setting up tiny doll homes and dressing them up and making them talk to each other, an idea came to me:

"Let's make cards for Grandma!"

"Yeah!" Emily and Caity both agreed.

"I'll write, 'I'll have a blue summer without you' on mine since she loves Elvis." I felt like I was being so creative. I started singing those words to the tune of the song, "*I'll have a blue....*"

"Don't say that, Hanna, it makes it seem like

she's dead," Emily, as the older cousin, corrected me.

A couple minutes later the phone rang, and my Aunt Liz answered it. Her "hello" was soon followed by a sudden burst of sobbing that I thought could only be fake. Until she told us the news, I honestly believed she was pretending, pulling a joke on us.

Aunt Liz came to Caity's room and we met her outside the door.

"Is she…?" Emily asked.

Aunt Liz just nodded, sniffling, as Emily wrapped her arms around her neck.

My mouth hanging wide open, the first tear trickled down my face. I didn't reach up to wipe it. Emily didn't know it, but she had been right.

Gambling

I go to Cleveland State which is in downtown Cleveland. It's less of a typical college campus and more of a row of university buildings on Euclid Avenue. It's a part of the city, so parking is expensive and fills up quickly in the university garages. I take the bus for my Tuesday and Thursday classes but on Mondays, Wednesdays, and Fridays, I come to campus straight from my tutoring job at a local Cleveland elementary school, so I need to find a parking space. I was paying two dollars a day to park at Trinity Cathedral across the street from the building where my class is, but then I was informed by my roommate that the Domain, the apartment building I lived in last year, just one block south of campus on Prospect Avenue, took their parking levers down and never tows or tickets. So I took a gamble and parked there one day, and felt victorious when I didn't get caught and henceforth parked there every time I drove to campus.

The day of the Indians home opener, a sold-out game and busy day downtown, I wasn't thinking and went with my usual parking space. After class, I got in my car only to have to get back out again, a little yellow paper tucked underneath my windshield wiper catching my attention. In messy, pencilled handwriting, the verdict was given: fifty dollars, twenty-five if I pay within fourteen days.

The worst thing that happens to a gambler is that he wins.

Grandma was unhealthy. Obese, diabetic, high blood pressure, shortness of breath, fluid retention, high cholesterol. But every time she went to the doctor, they told her that her heart was good. So she ran with that. She gave up on diets, reminding everyone that her heart was still healthy. But then it started fluttering, murmuring, beating out of rhythm.

The worst thing that happens to a gambler is that he wins.

Visit #6

Complete insanity and confusion, but there she was in the midst of it.

Two ten year olds were getting married. My dad was the officiant, and Aunt Natalie and my Grandma, wearing flowing purple dresses, did a dance routine on either side of the tiny bride and groom as they said their vows.

Quite a crowd showed up to watch these two minors become husband and wife, but instead of joining the packed sanctuary, I kept walking past the open doors. I found a place to sit down, where two boys from the middle school youth group that I'm in charge of came up to me and said that they liked the high school youth group better.

I don't know if this even counts as a visit. Maybe it was just an appearance, a teaser. But in a glimpse of purple, she was there.

Homelands

Closing in on Edinburgh, green hills dotted with brown cows rolling out endlessly on either side of us, my dad spoke of homelands.

I had already been in Europe for a couple weeks on my long-awaited study abroad trip to France with the French program at Cleveland State. Instead of flying home with the rest of my group, my dad picked me up Paris. After spending a day in the City of Lights, we drove in my dad's rental car to the ferry that took us across the English Channel, headed northwest to Liverpool as a part of the beatlemaniac pilgrimage, and from there we drove to Scotland.

While we were on the road, I asked my dad about Uncle Jeff, Grandma's youngest brother who had just died two weeks earlier after living with severe special needs his entire life. He was the first of Grandma's family to join her in eternity. Dad told me that he couldn't talk much and always referred to my Grandma as "Sissy" and even called my dad Sissy, as if he knew that he belonged to her. My dad predicted that if people have conversations in Heaven, the first thing Uncle Jeff would do is thank Grandma for always drinking after him, since when he would drink his pop, he would hardly drink any of it but would get his spit all over it in the process. Grandma didn't care and would always finish it for him.

When we crossed the border from England into Scotland, my dad proclaimed, "Your king has returned." He would go on to say this many more times throughout our drive.

"Oh my gosh…" I replied, shaking my head.

My dad glanced over at me from where he sits in the driver's seat on the right side of this backwards, English rental car. Sitting on opposite sides of the car is something I never got used to on this trip.

"What?" he asked incredulously. "I'm from here."

"No you're not, you're from America! Our ancestors are from here…" I rolled my eyes, repeating a conversation we had already had many times. "And, if they really were royalty, then they probably wouldn't have left in the first place."

Our family's heritage is mostly Anglo-Saxon, with Grandma's side of the family having a lot of Scottish ancestry. So naturally, my dad was pretty excited to visit Scotland, our homeland, and somehow believed that all the Scottish people would freak out that he was there and recognize the Scottish ancestry in us Americans, and treat my dad like a king.

We also spoke of another, more immediate homeland in our family: Alabama. For all his life and in the generations before, my dad's family has been making pilgrimages to the small southern towns of northern Alabama where most of their relatives lived. My mom told me that after every trip Grandma and her mother would take to Alabama, they would return with their voices completely gone, because of how much they talked, laughed, and sang while they were visiting their family.

Alabama came up because in my efforts to refute my dad's claims that he was Scotland's king, I mentioned that we don't even celebrate our European heritage; rather, we only ever talk about how our family is originally from the South. It also came up because I got big news while I was in France: after I graduate from college next year, I'm moving to Alabama.

We arrived as the sun began setting, checked into our Airbnb, and walked up Arthur's Seat, which according to Google is the number one thing to do in Edinburgh, and was also conveniently located right behind where we were staying. We even had a full view of it from the Airbnb's balcony.

After arriving at the base of the hill, my dad told me to go ahead because getting up the hill would be harder for him and he would take longer than me.

So I went. I got out my earbuds and listened to music as I made my way upwards, my calves starting to burn very quickly. I stopped often to look around and take pictures, trying to get one that would give this view justice when I got back home and showed people what Scotland looks like.

I arrived at the top and sat down at the edge of the cliff, scrolling through my music and tapping on the song "I Surrender" by Hillsong Worship. I had been praying over that song as I was awaiting news about my Teach for America acceptance and where I would be placed in the country. The wind blowing and tangling my hair, the setting sun piercing my eyes, the original homeland all around me, I sat there and continued to pray over those lyrics, thinking about my future in Alabama, *Lord, have Your way in me.*

My dad made it to the top and we stood and soaked it all in: the cityscape built on centuries of history that we can hardly fathom, the grass and surrounding hills a deep green that was rimmed with gold in the light of the setting sun. Everything looked golden from up there, until the hills and city reached the sea— then it was just blue. It was one of the most beautiful views I've ever beheld, definitely the most beautiful journey I've taken to get to a place. Most of the time when it comes to sightseeing, we drive, park in the parking lot, walk a little bit and take the picture.

You have to work to get this view, and it was so worth it.

The next day was June 25, 2018: the day that would have been Grandma's seventieth birthday.

Our time in Scotland was short because London was calling. We woke up and had to get going. To make the most of the time we had left in the homeland, we took the scenic route, driving along a road that lined up closely to the coast.

We didn't forget that it was Grandma's birthday. We listened to Elvis and ate chocolate bars as a tribute.

"I can't listen to this for very long," Dad said from the opposite side of the car, unwrapping his Mars bar. "It makes me too sad."

We stopped often, different views catching our attention and demanding that we get off the highway and look at it longer than we could see it as we were passing by in the car. Massive rocks jutting out of the water, ancient ruins dotting the rolling hills, the North Sea shimmering under the sun, the waters a deep blue like… well, like what? I'd love a good simile here but I can't find one. I guess I don't know because that was the kind of blue that sets the standard. From now on, if I see a blue like that again, I'm going to say that it's blue like the North Sea off the coast of Scotland.

As I bent down to find some shells and rocks

to take home to Amanda, my dad taking pictures of the sea with his iPhone, he remarked, "She'd be so excited that we're here."

I didn't have to ask who he was talking about. I stood up, sand-covered shells in my hand. "I think it's perfect that we're here on her birthday."

As we continued on the road towards London, I thought about our family's many homelands. Not even all of them are ancestral or based on where we've lived. Grandma wrote in her Jamaica journals upon arriving there for another vacation, "Back to the Homeland- 'Jamaica!'" (Grandma loved using quotation marks in her writing). It was a place she got to travel to with her daughter, and at the end of every trip there, she always wrote that she looked forward to the day when we all could go there together. She wasn't even from Jamaica, yet it was still a homeland to her because of the memories she had there, and the memories she hoped to make in the future.

I thought about homelands, and I wondered if our history is more strongly tied to people rather than places. Countries and cities serve as the settings for our stories while our families are actively writing them, our history unfurling as they live their lives, each generation starting the next chapter, every member carrying the words with them and passing them on. Homelands are fixed points, dots on a map, while people are mobile, carried around in your memories, hearts, and identities; because even though where you're from does play a part, it's ultimately your family who shapes you into you are. Scotland, Alabama,

Cleveland, and maybe even Jamaica— those are our homelands; but Grandma, the family that is here today, and the many generations that came before, they are our history.

So we wished Grandma a happy birthday from Scotland, our time spent there a chance to celebrate and pay tribute to her. And we got in the car, another journey to the homeland in store, another opportunity to learn our family's history, and to keep writing it.

Oprah

My mom probably got the call around the same time as Aunt Liz. Uncle Bill called Aunt Liz, my dad called my mom, each child designated to break the news to their spouses sitting at home, and from there it would go on to reach the rest of us.

In the midst of all of the doctors visits and hospitals stays that characterized the summer of 2008, Amanda started a journal for Grandma, just as Grandma had done for all of her grandkids, to tell them about the life that happened when they weren't around to see it.

Amanda watched Oprah every day and would write about it so Grandma, who didn't have a TiVo, could know what happened. In these journal entries, Amanda, who very well understood health problems and hospitals, would also encourage Grandma, telling her that even though it's hard, she could get through it.

The news was traveling around the family, bound to reach us wherever we were. It reached Grandma's four kids after they arrived back at her room, having had gone for a walk along those shiny and fluorescent hospital halls, thinking that everything was fine back at the room, that things were looking up. After it reached my mom when my dad called, it then reached Amanda as she was watching Oprah, ready to write in a journal that she'd never get to give to Grandma.

Dear Grandma,

Whenever I read a book, I imagine the layout of the characters houses like yours. It doesn't matter if it's a Jane Austen novel, Harry Potter, or poetry. If a character is in a kitchen, it looks likes yours. If they're walking up the stairs to their bedroom, the stairs and the bedroom all resemble the ones in your home.

I haven't been to that house in almost ten years. Today I went back.

I planned it all out with Caity and Aunt Natalie this morning at church. My dad was going to come but he decided to take a nap, but I also think he really didn't want to come. He said that there are too many memories there and then he went to his room.

We met at 3:15. I pulled into the driveway next door because that house is also vacant and I was too afraid of Mr. Wheeler seeing us from his house on the other side and calling the cops on us, something that you know he would definitely do. I wasn't being completely irrational and paranoid.

I ran to your house across the yards because I stupidly wore a pair of Toms (canvas shoes), having forgotten that there's currently snow on the ground. Caity and Joe were already there, so I ran right up the steps into the front door that Caity held open for me.

Coming at the house running, only focused on

getting out of the snow and through the door, I didn't have time to think about what I was doing, the significance of being back in this place for the first time in a long time. I didn't soak it all in until I caught my breath, standing in your empty living room. Rid of its old fluffy carpet, it felt brand new with its laminate tiles.

Caity, Joe, Amanda, Jake, and I did a complete walk through before Aunt Natalie and Isaiah got there, my feet cold and slightly numb from the snow that melted and soaked my shoes. You never got to meet Isaiah, the baby of all your grandkids.

Everything seemed smaller to me, your bedroom especially, even in all of its emptiness. I didn't feel afraid like I used to, always having the sneaking suspicion as a child that the house was alive. It's sad that the world shrinks as you get bigger and that when you grow up, everything loses the wonder and mystery it once held.

I went to look at the back door because there was something I was looking for, inspired by a shred of hope that I knew was impossible but held onto anyway.

When I went to Vacation Bible School in second grade with my friend Jewel, I made a wind chime as a craft, the skinny, golden chimes hanging from a plastic image of a smiling sun against a backdrop of a rainbow jutting out from voluminous clouds. Knowing that you loved wind chimes, there was never a moment that I thought it would be mine. I gave it to you on your birthday and you hung it on your back door.

Is it crazy that I thought there was a chance that it would still be there? I never got it when we were taking stuff from your house after you died. A ten year old's mistake.

What I found was not only the absence of the wind chime, but an entirely new back door.

But it's okay, because when we went into the basement, freshly cleaned but still smelling the same way it did when you lived there—like stale rags—we found Grandpa Kraker's old Cleveland Indians stickers stuck to the windows. Yellow and fading, bordered by the dirt and grime that accumulated on the windows after going years uncleaned, there was no mistaking that they were his. We peeled them off, the shape of them still evident, their vacancy leaving a clear spot amidst all the dirt, and Amanda pocketed them. Now they sit on my kitchen table, curling at the edges, but in their rightful place: in the family.

There was other evidence of our family's history in that house. On the closet door in one room, the logo of Rush drawn in pencil by Uncle Chris and a heart drawn by Aunt Natalie. In the middle bedroom, the measurement of Uncle Chris's height in 1988, recorded underneath an image of a cross carved into the wood. Buttercup the wooden horse still stands in the yard, sunken into the ground and surrounded by scraggly timber, but still there.

There was one time when I felt like I was walking through one of the books I've read rather than my family's old house. When I walked into Uncle Chris's old room, the room where Erik Von Newtonburg resides, my initial thought was, "It's Finch's room!", a character from a young adult novel, All the Bright Places, which I bawled my eyes out over when I finished reading it at four in the morning.

The entire house is updated, with fresh paint and new floors. This, along with the way it seemed so much smaller made it feel different, but it was being surrounded by family that put me in the right context. These people, even though so much time has passed and we've grown up and naturally grown apart a bit as we begin our lives, there are some things that will never be lost between us. Though the house is vacant and completely renovated and we're not the same little kids who want to play together and have sleepovers all the times, all of these places and experience are still ours. We can't get rid of them, and they can't get rid of us, even if we tried. After all, the house was standing there, empty and unlocked, as if it was waiting for us. It's like in a way, it's still ours. No one has lived there permanently since

Grandma. And even if someone were to move in, pieces of us still remain.

The people who walked through your house today are completely different than they were the last time they were here. Aunt Natalie got divorced from Uncle Joe, had Isaiah, and then got remarried to Carlos. Ten years later, some of your grandkids have become adults, and others are learning to drive and getting closer to finishing high school. The Joe that was there at your house with us was not your grandson, Caity's younger brother: it was her fiancé, soon to be husband. So there are going to be two Joes once again, even though Uncle Joe still comes around. We refer to him as "Funcle" Joe sometimes. The "f" stands for "former uncle." I know that would have made you laugh but also sad, because you really liked him.

Some of your other grandkids have boyfriends or girlfriends: Emily, Joe, Alyssa (except she recently broke up with hers) and Jake. This last one is recent news: my little brother has a girlfriend! His first one ever. I found out this week but he won't give me any details, and I'm kind of sad about it because I don't want him to have a girlfriend. It's not out of any kind of jealousy since I'm single and my younger brother is the one who has a significant other, it's just that I don't like seeing Jake grow up and act more like a man than a boy. But in the midst of all this, I'm trying to work on the whole serenity idea, you know, "God grant me the serenity to accept the things I cannot change." I'm sure you've heard of that before. I'm single, but you can still be excited for me because I love my life and the freedom that I have in this phase of my life, and I'm working on learning to be content in whatever circumstance.

We're all like your house. So much has changed, and so much hasn't. We're still Krakers, though some of our last names have changed or will be changing soon. We're still the same family, whose members are just going through the natural and inevitable phases of life. Growing, changing, breaking, updating. I just wish you were here, changing and yet staying the same right along with us.
Love,
Hanna Grace

Visit #4

A brief one, it lasted only seconds.

I was at the beach with friends, not at a Lake Erie beach but an ocean beach, probably in Florida. Something had happened that upset me—not sure what —and I stormed across the sand in anger.

I found one of those striped, cloth changing tents to stand behind and seethe, but I didn't get that far. Grandma popped out from behind it, and gave me a hug. She looked exactly as I remembered, her hug felt the same, only hurried.

There was only one difference: she had purple eyes. Her favorite color.

The color of the pant suit she wore when she renewed her vows to Grandpa Kraker after twenty-five years of marriage, the same pant suit she was buried in. The color of the ceiling she saw as she was dying, as my dad tells it, *she kept talking about a purple ceiling. A purple ceiling and a baby.*

The color of Heaven.

Seen and Unseen

Unraveling the cord, plugging it in, handing it to me so I can run the sweeper for her in the carpeted kitchen. Her mouth stood lightly agape, out or breath. Jake was standing in the doorway next to me, ready to help as well.

The hours she passed in solitude in that house, the years she lived alone there. Surrounded by emptiness and quiet, save for the squirrel rustling around upstairs and the sound of the T.V. She was just one person, but her heart was so big that it took up all those rooms, it filled the emptiness. It flowed through the pipes and the cracks under the doors. You couldn't meet her, have a conversation with her, see how she loved others, and not see the heart within her. It was impossible to miss.

My dad, 21-years-old, pulling out of the driveway, putting his foot on the gas, prepared to stay that way for the next eight hundred miles until Lakeland, Florida, on his way to begin his education at Southeastern College. Grandma stood in the doorway the entire time, watching, unblinking. As he got further down the street, she moved out of the doorway onto the steps, waving until he was out of sight.

Her bathroom drawer, empty save for the eyelash curler that mystified me as a little girl. I played with it like it was a weapon, rather than something for beauty, not realizing it could actually be both.

Her pregnant belly, young face.

The mattress on the floor in the piano room at Uncle Joe and Aunt Natalie's house. This is where Grandma slept after Aunt Natalie had Zoey and Grandma stayed with her for awhile to help with the newborn. The mattress stayed there, ready for when Grandma would get out of the hospital and couldn't be on her own just yet.

Uncle Bill's CD release concert for his long-awaited first solo album, *Russellville.* One of the songs, *Green Grass of Home,* is about him and Grandma looking out at her backyard: *she said I know it looks nice and this might sound crazy, but I can't help missing the way it used to be.* My dad plays GiGi's old acoustic guitar and Uncle Bill sings about this moment spent with his mom, the images of his childhood spent at that house. I try to fathom how proud she would have felt that night listening to him perform these songs that he's worked so hard on, and my heart hurts in the effort because it's impossible to conjure a feeling as intense and overwhelming as a mother's love and pride for her child. I know she would have been crying, though, the tears streaming down, her hand reaching up to wipe them away. Especially when he played this song.

My dad sings of streets of gold, that she's dancing down them. I believe this, though I have one more thing to add: she dances, and she never runs out of breath.

Dear Grandma,

I just wanted to tell you what Amanda said today. My semester starts next week so I'm enjoying these last couple days of summer while they're here, though having this much down time is driving me a little crazy. I need to learn how to relax and how to be okay with having days off. I've been hanging out with Amanda to spend more time with her before I go back to living at my Lakewood apartment full time. Today, we rode our bikes around our neighborhood and stopped at the community pool.

While swinging on the swings outside of the pool gate, Amanda said that she wishes she could ride her trike over to your house and see you.

When Presley was little, Aunt Natalie told me that he would say all the time that he wished he could take a rocket ship to Heaven to see you.

But unfortunately, the sidewalks don't go all the way to your house and Center Road is too dangerous with its excessive amounts of traffic and semi trucks for Amanda to ride her trike, and rocket ships don't go to Heaven.

Two weeks ago I went to Chicago with Kayla to see Hamilton, a hip-hop musical about Alexander Hamilton. It sounds unusual but I bet you would've liked it. We've been obsessed with the soundtrack and the travel bug has bitten me so hard that getting tickets for seventy-two dollars to the always-sold-out musical and *getting to take a trip to Chicago seemed like a good deal to me.*

Our seats were nosebleeds and we were exhausted from leaving Brunswick at six a.m., driving to Chicago and spending all day walking around sightseeing, but the show was amazing. I got chills throughout the entire thing, as expected. What I didn't expect was how much it would impact me emotionally. As I get older, I cry more easily over movies, songs, videos on Facebook, and other stuff like that. I blame my mom.

The first time I cried was when Aaron Burr and Alexander Hamilton sing "Dear Theodosia" to their newborn children, as I thought about how much my parents love me and how blessed I am to have been raised by them.

The second time I cried was when Alexander's son, Philip died.

The third time I cried was during the finale when the actors sang the last song, "Who Lives, Who Dies, Who Tells Your Story," together. The whole premise of the song is summed up by George Washington when he sings, "You have not control who lives, who dies, who tells your story." We have no control that Alexander Hamilton died, that his wife lived, that Lin Manuel Miranda wrote a hip hop musical about him over two hundred years later and that's how his story and legacy have been told.

I cried because even though I've been writing to you, writing about you, and even though I got a lot of positive feedback about all this writing which was originally my senior research project, I have felt hesitant about what I could do with this. My dream is to write and publish a book, and after I gave my dad the finished product of my project, all ninety-six pages though the requirement was only twenty, he said that this was it. This thing I've started, that I've been toying with, the project that got me an A, is the book idea I've been waiting for. Both my professor and my dad validated the dream within me that I didn't dare speak out loud. But still, I never thought I could write much more than the ninety-six pages, that the ten years I had with you are already so limited and wouldn't offer me much more material for me to write about and turn into a book.

But sitting there, listening to the song, I vowed that I would see this project through, that I would write this book, that I would learn to be okay with being vulnerable and share this with the world in any way that I can. We can't control that you died or that the rest of us have lived, but I can control if I tell your story. And I'm going to. I'm going to, because even though the sidewalks end before we can get to your house and even though rocket ships can't take us to Heaven to visit you, we still have our memories, our stories, and the words, and that's how we can get

to you.
Love,
Hanna Grace

McDonalds

When there's a death in the family and kids need to be taken care of while the adults get a handle on the situation, McDonalds was the temporary place for us to go. My Aunt Liz's dad, Mr. Pick, pulled into their gravel driveway and we were instructed to go with him.

As I walked out the door, I was met by a crying Amanda and my mom walking up the front path. Sniffling and not wiping away her tears, Amanda hugged me around my waist.

"It's gonna be okay, Hanna, it's gonna be okay," she said in my ear, though it seemed like more of a message to herself since she was the one crying.

Emily, Caity, Joe, my brother, and I climbed into Mr. Pick's car. I remember the seat being tan leather and the car being impeccably clean. Emily took the front seat and the rest of us shared the back seat. I was concerned that there were four kids and only three seat belts, but I didn't say anything.

We went to the Strongsville McDonalds on Pearl Road, and ate our happy meals while sitting at one of the booths that are meant to look like they're classic and from the fifties. I could see the twisty slides of the play place through the glass doors on the other side of the restaurant, the cubby holes with Ronald McDonald smiling at us and telling us to take our shoes off in his speech bubble, but none of us went in. We just sat there quietly, eating our french fries one by one, the same food she always loved to eat, the food she'd have in her hand as she walked up our driveway.

Ten Years Later

There are two ways I wish I could write. Alone and quietly is one way; heart-swellingly spectacular is the other. Basically, I wish I could write the way that the end of *The Lion King* makes you feel: the orchestral music building as Simba marches up Pride Rock in slow motion, the rightful king roaring at the sky, the rain quenching the fire that just raged a couple scenes ago. But we can't always get what we want, and things don't always go to plan: shortly after I planted myself on the deck to write, Amanda came out the back door with our Great Dane, Brinks (talking to him as usual), with her iPad blaring African gospel music. In addition, I shouldn't waste my time trying to be like Disney, because they have made about a million blockbuster movies and now they have a theme park with a castle and its own zip code, and on top of that they own Star Wars and Marvel, so we all have a long way to go to be like them.

Actually, there's a third way I wish I could write: perfectly, or at least close to it. I just want the words to be enough to encompass what I feel after ten years— ten years to the day since I last saw my grandma alive.

I can sit here hoping for all my writing wishes to come true, but it would be contrary to my experiences. These ten years have not been quiet or alone, and they haven't always been heart-swellingly spectacular; sometimes they were one or or the other, sometimes they were neither. Ten years definitely haven't been Disney nor were they perfect— no where close to it.

Ten years had its quiet moments, like those long summer days when we're bored but won't admit that we're ready for school to start again, and those family parties when you look around and realize that we're all growing up and we spend a little too much time on our phones, sending snapchats and scrolling through Facebook and Instagram, mostly likely seeing the same posts we saw earlier that day but we keep looking anyways. But for the most part, in our family, these ten years have been loud: the Kraker Brothers playing at a gig, the kids screaming and chasing each other in circles as they pass through the doors that connect the kitchen to the living room to the den, and back around again. It has been the sound of us cheering on Jake at his wrestling matches, Shannon at her softball games, the sound of Aunt Natalie screaming as she saw Caity's left hand with an engagement ring on it for the first time.

The ten years have never passed alone. We're all still here.

There have been spectacular moments, times when my heart-swelled. Christmas day 2008, the year Grandma died, Aunt Kelly announced some joyous news: she was pregnant and a new baby would be joining our family in July. Dancing with my cousins to *December, 1963* by Franki Valli and the Four Seasons at Carlos and Aunt Natalie's wedding, seeing Joe and Caity, who had just started dating, still getting to know each other and completely on cloud nine, dancing together. Telling old family stories, hearing about how Grandma would start screaming and going crazy with excitement when her brother Dan would announce his arrival by honking his horn all the way down the street, getting out of his car with a box of pizza to share. Sometimes just laughing and talking together, reminiscing and feeling nostalgic for a time when you weren't even alive yet, is enough to fill your heart with joy.

And these past ten years haven't been perfect, because it's been ten years of life, and life is never perfect.

Ten years definitely aren't Disney. This hasn't been a ninety minute fairy tale that has its troubles but always finds that happy ending, the princess finding her prince, the villain defeated. Ten years ago, the happy ending was hinged on one person, and that person was checked into the Cleveland Clinic, and a couple days later her heart stopped beating after her kids had stepped out of the room to take a walk.

August 15, 2018: here we are, ten years later. Uncle Bill's fiftieth birthday, a hot summer day that I spent at the Cleveland Metroparks Zoo with my friend Jenna. I didn't think that going to the zoo with Jenna would lead to such an emotional day for me: seeing the lions made me want to watch *The Lion King* (naturally), and going to the Australia exhibit tapped into the deep wanderlust deposits in my soul and made me want to hop on the next flight and see the Outback for myself. After dropping off Jenna, I did what I could to fulfill my wishes at the zoo, and I watched *The Lion King* with Amanda. And I cried when the prophetic baboon Rafiki told Simba that his dad, Mufasa, isn't really gone because "he lives in you" and when Mufasa appeared in the clouds to the distressed Simba, commanding him to "Remember who you are." The movie was good. As for my Australia wishes, I unfortunately cannot afford the airfare.

My family may not have gotten our happy ending in the typical Disney fashion. That Grandma, that mother, sister, and friend, piano player, Christ-follower who I last saw ten years ago today sitting on that patio couch at my Uncle Bill's birthday party, did not survive. We did get a Lion King ending though: just as Mufasa dies but lives on through Simba, so Grandma died but lives on through us. We just have to remember who we are: we are Krakers, descended from that one seed who is invisible once again, but is still visible because she lives in us. For the past ten years and the next ten, in the quiet and alone times, when life isn't especially heart-swelling or spectacular, when life keeps being imperfect, when that Disney happy ending is elusive as ever, we still carry on, remembering who we are.

Dear Grandma,

I'm at the time in my life when everyone asks me what my plans are and what I want to do in my future. I answer, telling them that I'm an English and French major at Cleveland State. And I already know what's coming next, because nearly every time without fail, they ask me what exactly it is that I plan to do with those two degrees.

The unrealistic answer is get a million-dollar book idea, write the book, and then once it's a bestseller, do everything in my power to forbid Hollywood from destroying it with a crap movie, and then travel and read and write more books for the rest of my life. And of course gives lots of money away and serve God and love Him with all of my heart, soul, mind. I also hope that God has an amazingly handsome and intelligent and godly man in store for me and that we'll have some amazingly gorgeous and intelligent and godly children together. This wish list could keep going on and on but those are the main things.

The realistic answer that I decided on about a year ago is teacher, at least until all of that book stuff happens. It really would mesh well with the traveling lifestyle that I'd like to have. I made this decision after getting a second job tutoring at an elementary school in Cleveland's inner-city and finding a purpose and passion in helping students. Before that,

I was planning on going into ministry as a career. But my internship at church has not been the experience I was hoping for, and I changed my mind. I just can't live forever where church is my place of work rather than simply my church, always feeling the pressure about the number of kids and planning all of the events. After I told Doc about my job with Teach for America in Alabama and that I'll be leaving my internship, he congratulated me, but also told me that he'd love to see me working in the church again one day. So I won't close that door completely and maybe I'll work in ministry in a different capacity.

Whatever happens, what I know for sure is that I don't want to live a quiet life. I don't want to waste the time that I've been given by playing life safely. I want to do something important, I want to go places, I want to help people, I want to show the love of God to the world. Sometimes, when I've spent too much time scrolling through Instagram, it seems like the only way to do this is to become famous or start nonprofits or support about a million different causes. But I know that's not true, because sometimes it's the lives that appear to be the most simple that are the least quiet.

I know this by looking at your life. Your seemingly ordinary life was anything but quiet: you lived loud, and loved louder. Your impact resounds.

You lived in Brunswick, Ohio, a place no one

*has ever heard of unless they're from around here.
You worked at the phone company and taught piano.
You got married, had four kids, went to church every
Sunday, lived in a house with a backyard, and you
had a dog, a poodle named Bo. You lived the typical
American life, but you weren't typical.*

*I can't fathom the amount of people you
impacted, in all areas of your life. At work, I can
imagine you cheering up the people on the other side
of the phone, maybe even being the only kind person
they talked to that day. And even though you worked
at the phone company, I think your real life's work
and your true passion was ministry. You dedicated
your life to guiding people in the faith at both of your
churches, volunteering your time and talents joyfully.
Your obituary even states that your favorite thing to
do was worship God, the very thing that you are now
spending your time doing for all eternity. As the
matriarch of our family, you showed us love, patience,
endurance, thoughtfulness, generosity, and led us in
faith.*

*Tonight I went back to the House of the Lord
and took Amanda (who turned thirty-one yesterday)
and Jake along with me. The worship was so
energetic as everyone danced, clapped, and jumped
around, and I thought that the sermon was really
good as well. The pastor came out of Hebrews, one of
my favorite books of the Bible, chapter 12 verses 1-3,*

a verse that I'm sure you were familiar with: "Therefore, since we are surrounded by such a great cloud of witnesses, let us throw off everything that hinders and the sin that so easily entangles. And let us run with perseverance the race marked out for us, fixing our eyes on Jesus, the pioneer and perfecter of faith. For the joy set before him he endured the cross, scorning its shame, and sat down at the right hand of the throne of God." The verse from the mission trip this past summer, the verse that's the subject of a sermon by Christine Caine that I watch all the time.

It wasn't anything like I expected though: Bishop Joey wasn't there, the service only lasted forty minutes (unlike when I'd go with you on Sunday mornings and it would last two hours), and it was held in a smaller sanctuary space.

It was completely different than what I thought it would be, but I still loved it. I want to go back.

I want to go back so I can talk to Bishop Joey and so I can sit in that sanctuary, surrounded by people who knew you and were impacted by you. People who I don't know, yet I'm connected to because of you.

Everywhere, there are people who will never forget you, people who were encouraged by your love, embraced by your kindness. You're a person who's impossible to forget. And I'm sure it wasn't easy to be kind all the time, to show love to everyone, but you did it anyway. You were even able to show grace to your ex-husband, as my dad says he never heard you say one bad thing about him. You laughed at my jokes that weren't funny, you were welcoming to everybody, you kept all of those journals for each of your grandkids, you wrote encouraging notes to your pastors every week and to many other people, even the chef and waiter at the resort you stayed at in Jamaica. You put on a brave face until the very end.

If I listen close, I can hear it.

As I drive, Amanda almost falling asleep the back seat, Jake talking to me about his friends, I can hear it. Your influence still reverberating, resonating. I look around at the people who knew you, I look at my family, and I still hear your life, softly in the background, refusing to be silenced. It's imprint is still audible, still working, still extraordinary. You never really will be gone, not as long as we remember, as we continue to respond to and be influenced by the person you were.

Thank you for refusing to live a quiet life, because your example has inspired me to do the same. I know that I can live an unquiet life from Cleveland, Ohio, and later on, from Alabama. The place I'm at, the status I have—all of that doesn't matter. It's about living fully the life God has given me and every day being sustained and transformed by the work of Christ in my soul. It's all about Him, and only Him.

An unquiet life. I can hear it now.
Love,
Hanna Grace

Prayers, Toasts, and MySpace

Thanksgiving Day, 2018. My dad said the prayer, my mom said the toast. The prayer was short, full of thanks as any Thanksgiving prayer—scratch that—as *any* prayer should be. He thanked God for family, for all of the unbelievable blessings we have as Americans living in the first world, for the newly founded family standing in our midst, Joe and Caity.

Together, we said, "Amen," and together we raised our glasses. The adults had wine, the kids plastic cups full of sparkling cider.

"To the Kraker family," My mom looked away, trying to regain composure, as her eyes were already welling up with tears. She cleared her throat, "I love you all."

And we all took a sip, except me. My mom and my eyes had met in that moment, and I teared up because I could tell she was about to start crying. I raised my glass, but didn't take a sip until I swallowed my tears.

By googling her name, I recently discovered that my grandma had a MySpace. Her username was "grammiekraker." I was too young to have MySpace when it was in its prime so I don't really know how it worked, but after browsing my Grandma's page, it seems like it was a means of sharing your pictures. No posting statuses or sharing posts, like Facebook.

Her profile picture is her holding newborn Shannon. All the rest of her photos are of her with her family, or just of her family. The captions read like this: *my brother dan. my brother paul. my brother don. alyssa and grammie. my amanda. my grandkids. Chris & his family,* and so on and so forth. She didn't miss anybody. It's like she made sure to get everybody on there, to use this platform to share the people who meant the most to her. Today, social media has become extremely superficial and people put a lot of time and effort that would probably be a lot more productive elsewhere in their lives into finding the perfect caption and choosing to post the picture that will get the most likes. I think that my Grandma used social media in a much better way by posting what she liked, not worried about how others would respond, and sharing content that gave an accurate representation of real life and real people.

Through prayers, toasts and MySpace, both my parents and Grandma confirmed that our faith in God and our love for our family are what give our life meaning. Though life can change in an instant, those are the things that are forever, the things for which we can always be thankful and raise a glass.

Praying

Back at Uncle Bill and Aunt Liz's house, after eating a Happy Meal and not going in the PlayPlace, Caity and I went to the tree house.

"Let's write a song for Grandma," I suggested, even though I wasn't particularly musical. It was like a part of me wanted to worship, maybe because I knew that's what Grandma would do. Through the highs and lows, she worshipped.

"Yeah, like Camp Rock," she replied as she swung underneath a tree branch. This idea never made it past the talking stages and we never actually wrote a song.

Everyone congregated at the house, trickling in one-by-one. The kids mostly stayed outside.

My Aunt Natalie got out of her car inconsolable, pulling at the hem of her shirt as tears streamed down her face, sniffling, her lips trembling, unable to speak.

Doc, our pastor, pulled in. He walked down the gravel driveway in his cowboy boots, and called all of the kids in the backyard over to him. He told us to join hands, and he prayed for us.

Inside, there was a circle of mourners on benches and chairs, every aunt and uncle, her brothers, Doc. No one turned on the lights in the living room, so as the sun set, the room steadily became darker and darker. The only light filtered in from the dining room, silhouetting the blotchy, tear-stained faces. Most people looked down at the floor, but I remember my Uncle Chris, dabbing his eyes with tissues and staring right ahead.

I walked to the back window, past the brown bag full of our peaches on the kitchen counter, and looked outside at the porch. I found the bench she had been sitting on at Uncle Bill's birthday party, the last time I saw her. I stared at that red cushion, locking into my mind the creases, the sag in the middle.

Praying, praying, and more praying. That was all we could do.

Things Haven't Been the Same

Since Grandpa died. Seven months after I was born, he died in November 1998 after fighting the cancer that had sprung up unexpectedly over the summer. That's when Grandma stopped writing in the journal she started for me. She wrote to me that she never fully adjusted to her identity as a widow.

"I think she was depressed," guesses my mom. "Towards the end, she always minimized the amount she'd have to walk. When she went to Master Pizza, she'd park her car right on the curb in front of the door."

I never would have guessed sadness or depression based on her smile, based on the way she laughed at the things I said, but that's just the perspective I had since I only knew her in my childhood. Until the end, at least how ten-year-old me saw it, she put others first, her problems later on. I don't remember Grandpa Kraker, though his picture rests on my top of my headboard. I don't remember Grandma as a sad person, though I can recognize the loneliness now. And still, all of this led to August

20th, a day I remember very well, and things haven't been the same

Since Grandma died. A person dying changes a family totally and irreversibly. Mourning dawns, not only for the people but the things about their existence that you took for granted. We don't spend Christmas morning at her house anymore and we can only hear her play piano through recordings. Grandma said that she couldn't wait to watch us walk down the aisle, but she didn't even make it to see us walk to get our diplomas, and things will never be the same again in our family. They never could be, because she isn't here and she was once a concrete fixture in our lives, her hugs always waiting, that white explorer always pulling into the driveway, a seat, a ticket always reserved for her because she always showed up even when it was hard, and things haven't been the same

Because that's what happens when people leave and grief enters the picture. No matter how much time passes, you never really stop missing people. And even that grief, that missing feeling hasn't stayed the same: it's no longer as fresh as it was in the face of her sudden death tens years ago, as forcefully present as it was in adjusting to life without her. It has now evolved into a constant thing, dully hovering in the background, a part of life. This grief rises and falls, becoming more poignant at certain points on the calendar: another birthday, another holiday that she isn't here to celebrate with us. A day like today, August 20th, 2018, the tenth anniversary of her death, is the most poignant day of all, and things haven't been the same

Except for one thing.

As is the custom on every August 20th, I went through the bottom drawer of my dresser today, and as is the usual occurrence, I cried a lot. I picked up the polka-dotted scarf that she put over my carseat when she drove me around when I was a baby, and I tried it on, trying to find a way to wear it fashionably. None of them worked, and that's probably because the scarf really belongs in the drawer. I read all of the birthday cards she gave me, all saying the same thing, "I am so proud of you and I love you—Grammie", but still all so special. The waterworks were strongest when I read the journal Grandma wrote for me.

I see the same things each June 25th and August 20th that I go through the drawer, but something different sticks out to me every time. Today, a funeral card with her name, the dates of her birth and death underneath a picture of a bridge on the front, and a prayer on the back are what grabbed my attention. The prayer said that "on this day, God rescued you."

Rescued.

In the midst of grief it is our inclination to get mad at God, to look at the situation and see only how it affects us. We can shake our fists towards the sky, angry that Grandma was taken away from us. We say that those we mourn are in a better place; but even so, we are selfish because we'd rather that they be here with us. What we need to do instead is look at the circumstance in a different way and in what is probably the correct way: she was rescued. Because even as we're crying ten years later, as we're looking around and seeing all the ways that things haven't been the same, if we would just clear our eyes and thoughts and take a step back and really look at things, we see that one very sure, one very solid thing hasn't changed at all and in fact, could never change, and that is God. He is the only constant, the only thing that stays the same, and just as He rescued Grandma who, as she told my dad, just wanted to lay down and die, so He rescues us, His everlasting and glorious sameness that spans yesterday, today, and forever comforting and stabilizing us in the face of life's fragility.

As I sit around the dinner table with my family on the day that Grandma was rescued ten years ago, reminiscing, listening to my dad tell stories of how tough Grandpa Kraker was; how everyone used to live in that house at one time or another when my dad and his siblings were newly married; how Grandma and Grandpa always fought and Amanda would go hide because they yelled so much, but they always made up in the end; I can tell, things haven't been the same, but that's okay. It's okay because there's always going to be a reason to cry, there's always going to be those days when you mourn the way life used to be, when you miss someone's physical presence; but *thank God*, thank Him that He stays the same, that He rescues, and that He wipes our tears and comforts those who mourn.

Visit #7

Sitting on a wooden bench during a church service in Mwiciringiri, Kenya, surrounded by the sound of worship in Kikuyu being sung and the pounding of a drum and a metal ring, a little girl of about three years old climbed onto my lap.

I turned to the nine-year old boy, Simon, sitting next to me. He was old enough that he had already started learning English in school and could understand basic words and phrases. "What's her name?" I asked, pointing at this girl on my lap, who was now grabbing my earrings, poking the tattoo on my wrist, mystified.

After a couple seconds, Simon replied, "Christine."

I turned to her, smiling, "Sasa, Christine." I took in her dirty fingernails, her dusty tennis shoes whose velcro was coming undone, her pink sweater that had two buttons on each shoulder. Later on in the service, she fell asleep in my lap and while lost in her deep slumber, she peed on me.

That night I fell asleep quickly, still exhausted

and jet-lagged from the fourteen hour flight from New York to Nairobi. I fell asleep, and Granda visited me.

She was sitting in her living room, smiling, surrounded by crumpled up papers and wrappers. Content. Her couch had been moved to block the doorway to the kitchen, the only light filtering from the big window facing the backyard.

I moved across the living room to sit next to her, and for the first time in all of her visits to me since she died, she spoke to me.

"I read your book," she said as she turned towards me on the couch.

Naturally, I freaked out, shifting around on the couch, my mouth falling open in surprise, struggling to find the words to say. "What? I wanted it to be a surprise! How did you even get a copy of it?"

She smiled, then replied, "Luke sent it to me."

"What—" I began, baffled that one of my friends from church had sent it to her when he knew nothing about the book in the first place.

She kept going, "He thought I should know about it."

In that moment, I noticed her sweater. It was yellow, with two buttons on each shoulder.

And that's where our visit ended. I didn't get to go any further, didn't get to ask the pressing questions, didn't get to hear what she thinks of all of this. But I do know that she knows about it, and that she says so with a smile.

Dear God,

Thank You for water.

Something about water compels me to pray. It was on the shores of Lake Erie that I gave my life to You after a week at camp on Kelley's Island and a lifetime of Sundays spent in your church. I often park my car at Rocky River Park or Edgewater, stare at the waves and the Cleveland skyline in the distance and pray, for anyone and anything. I listen to the words of the worship songs I play on my phone in the background, and sometimes I just sit there and think about Your love and goodness, sometimes crying because it can be overwhelming.

The water I was baptized in as You were. The water that gives me life. The water that falls from the sky, ushering in spring, rinsing the salt from the icy winter that covered my car.

While it's where I find You, water hasn't always been a good sign in my life.

The water that dripped from her navel, as she recounted in the journal my dad read aloud as we sat in a circle in her empty living room and listened. The wheelchair she used, her feet and legs swollen from fluid retention. That coupled with diabetes, obesity, a heart that beat out of rhythm, and ultimately, kidney failure, she died. IV needles pumping water into her veins, water leaking from her skin, she was welcomed into glory, walking on streets of gold under a purple *ceiling, a baby in the distance.*

So here I am, nearly ten years later, at Wendy Park. Or at least, trying to get to Wendy Park. Siri on my iPhone took me directly to the address of the park, which means that rather than taking me to the entrance, it took me North down West 25th, through the Lakeview Estates housing projects, and through the gravelly, industrial roads that line the North Coast, prime real estate left to factories and water treatment plants, an endless assembly line of semi trucks carrying salt and rocks coming around the corner. Every time I looked up, another truck was rounding the bend, heading towards me.

It was going to be perfect, too. I was going to lean against the fence that keeps me and others from jumping, that used to have the yellow toxic signs posted, the skull with crossbones warning of the polluted water below. I was going to look at where the river meets the Lake, the river that once burned but is now freezing cold, freshly fallen snow covering the ground on this second day of spring. But instead, I sit behind the wheel of my red Volkswagen Beetle, mad at my phone, staring at chain link fences posting the words Private Property, *leaving me with nowhere to go but the way I came.*

And here I am, a really busy and tired college student, lost in Cleveland who scorns the ten year old girl she used to be for not caring more, for not making the most of the time she had. For not remembering more words, for giving into fear of ghosts rather than spending more time at the house that was only ten minutes away.

She was only ten minutes away. But I was only ten years old. And now I'm ten years away, the memories rusty, her voice unclear. I've moved and changed and she has stayed the same: gone.

So today, I pray a prayer that is unlike my usual ones. While I don't view You as a genie who grants my wishes, today I come to You with a request.

Please tell my grandma that I say hi.

That I wish I cared more about that word when she was still there for me to say it to. That I wish I could have counted how many times I said it. I imagine that I said it thousands of times to her in the ten years that I knew her. That I wish I said each "hi" with meaning, never simply saying "hey" or just waving.

Please tell her that I say hi, and that I say it with a smile, with tears, and with arms outstretched, ready to complete the embrace that awaits me years from now in Heaven.

Can I add more than just hi, please?

Please tell that I miss her. That I've never harbored such grief as the grief I feel for the grandmother I knew, and the girl, woman, teenager, that I never got to know.

Tell her that I wish to change my appearance a lot, just like any person does, but make sure to tell her that there's one thing I've never wished to change: my eyes, because I share them with her.

Tell her that I'd give up listening to the Beatles if it meant that I could hear her play piano again, and I'd never regret that decision.

Tell her that she's the kind of strong, faithful, genuinely kind woman that I hope to be. That I write about her, think about her, that I'm so thankful for when she visits me, and that I wish she'd come again soon.

Something about water compels me to pray. I always find there's more for me to say, confess, reflect on. But out of all the things I just said, only one word really matters: hi.

It's the start of a conversation that we'll get to continue once we're reunited in eternity.

and he will make your paths straight.

Crooked Meets Great

River meets lake.

River winds through forests and cities and curves relentlessly, giving itself the name of Crooked River. The avenue of industry, it carries ships and barges beneath bridges and around the bends under a smog-filled sky, somehow finding its way to the Great Lake, and from there, its goes to the ocean. The river doesn't rush into the lake. There's no urgency: brown meets blue, crooked meets great, no battle, no struggle, no pushback. They just come together.

And so granddaughter meets grandmother.

Granddaughter runs through the yard, through the house, from watching the TV to playing with dolls to sledding down snowy hills with cousins, to blowing out the candles on the birthday cake, and somehow, amidst all her running and playing and carefree life, she finds herself running into the arms of her Grandma, where she sits on the rocking chair, the bench at church, her rollator, her couch. Granddaughter grows up, gets taller, laughs, cries, and learns, always changing. Grandma is always there, watching and waiting, always patient, always gracious.

It's a miracle that the river find its way, that it twists its way to its destination, to a greater body, because for a while it seems like it never will. The river seems perfectly content to keep winding, taking turns at sharp angles, subjected to never reaching its destination even though its right there. It's so close.

Granddaughter forgets where she's going, forgets her destination and instead likes to meander, to make things way more complicated than they need to be. She forgets that Grandma is closer than she thinks, that she can stop winding, stop turning, and look around. Look at the piano, the red marks she left on the keys from her manicures, the packet of Juicy Fruit on display in the check-out line at Giant Eagle. She finds her by looking out the window as she drives by her house on the way to church, by listening to an Elvis song, being told that she looks like her, even sounds like her sometimes. On June 25, on August 20, on Thanksgiving, Christmas, birthdays, when Doc stands before the congregation and talks about a beautiful woman who used to send him a note every week, thanking him for his sermons and encouraging him. In the smiles of her brothers when they come to visit, through these dreams. By looking at the cross. Remembering whose she is and who she is with.

I turn and there she is, stretched out like a

great lake against a blue horizon, stretching from west to east, heading north into the sky. Undeniable, unavoidable. She seems to be gone and unreachable, but she's still there.

River meets Lake. The crooked find its way to the great.

Isn't that how it goes? The crooked shall be made straight.

And so granddaughter meets grandmother.

Acknowledgments

Hi, Grandma. I don't know what else I can say but that you're the reason for this. You're gone but you're not, because you're still inspiring and mentoring me. I don't care if two people or two thousand people read this book, I just care that your story is told.

Mom and Dad, I love you both so much that my heart hurts. Thank you for all of your undying support and encouragement. I never doubt that you'll be there for me and help me as I pursue my goals and dreams. Mom, it's your turn to write a book! Dad, finish the album!

To the greatest professor at Cleveland State University, thank you so much, Ted. You were the first person to call this a book when it was just supposed to be a twenty-page research project. This book never would have happened if not for your guidance and advice, and if not for your writing classes at CSU that taught me so much and developed me as a writer.

Thank you Rachel for the beautiful cover

design (I'm seriously in love!) and for reading my manuscript early on and supporting me so much throughout this project. Also, thank you for your friendship. It means so much to me.

Thank you, Jen Keirn. You give the realest advice and I'm so thankful for all that you've told me about what it takes to write and publish a book (hustle!) and just to be a writer.

Thank you, Cleveland. You are the greatest city in the world and I'm blessed to call you my hometown.

Thank you, Elvis. It just feels right to thank you, too.

Thank you to Amanda and Jake (Krakpot on Soundcloud— go listen) for being the greatest siblings in the world. Thank you, Kayla, for being my best friend and always being supportive and believing in this book. And thank you, Michele, for reading this book when it was at its 96-page stage and for encouraging me to finish it and publish it— that impacted me more than you know.

And finally: thank You, Jesus. I could not live this life without You. You are my purpose, the reason I am living and breathing every day, my peace, my joy, my source of fulfillment and contentment, my savior. Thank You for what you did in the life of my grandma, and for what You're doing every day in mine. You change everything. For the rest of my days I will thank You.

About the Author

Hanna is a recent graduate of Cleveland State University where she received her BA in Creative Writing and French. She currently teaches English in Alabama. This is her first book. You can find her on Instagram @hannakraker.

Before you go, Hanna wants to share what she tells her students with anyone who reads this: believe in the power of your words and your perspective. Keep writing and keep going. You're not done.

Made in the USA
Las Vegas, NV
09 August 2021